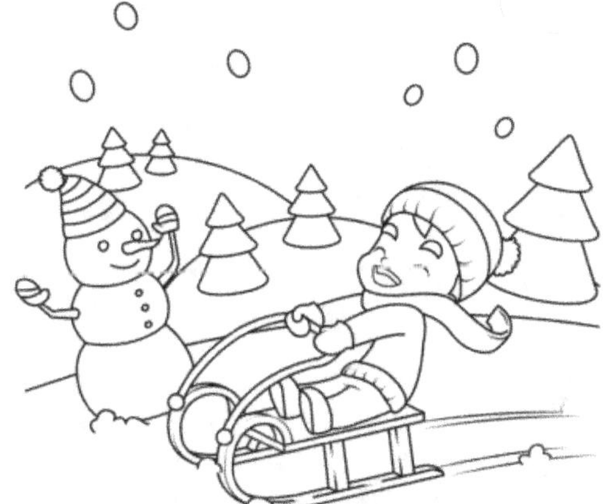

Winter

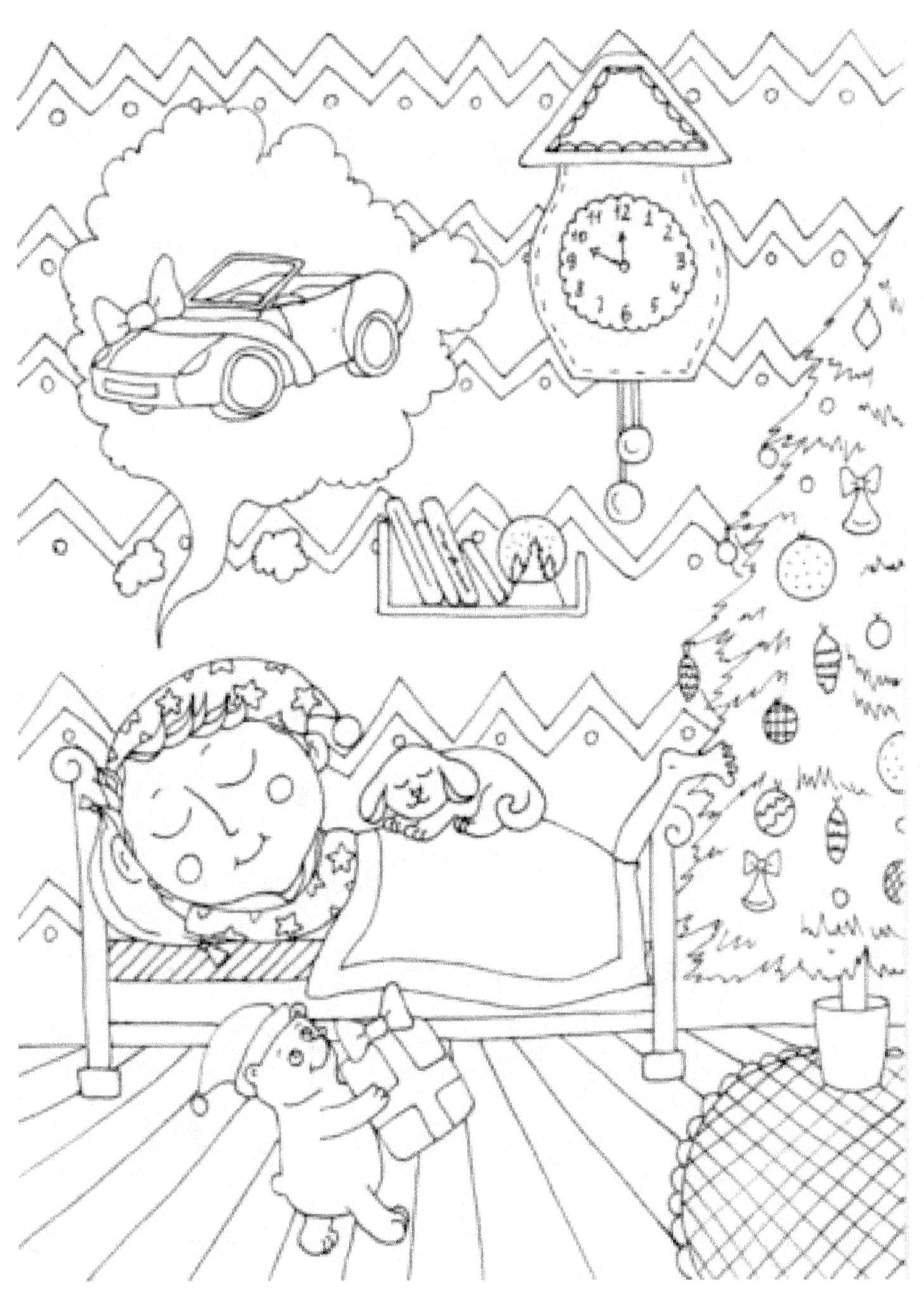

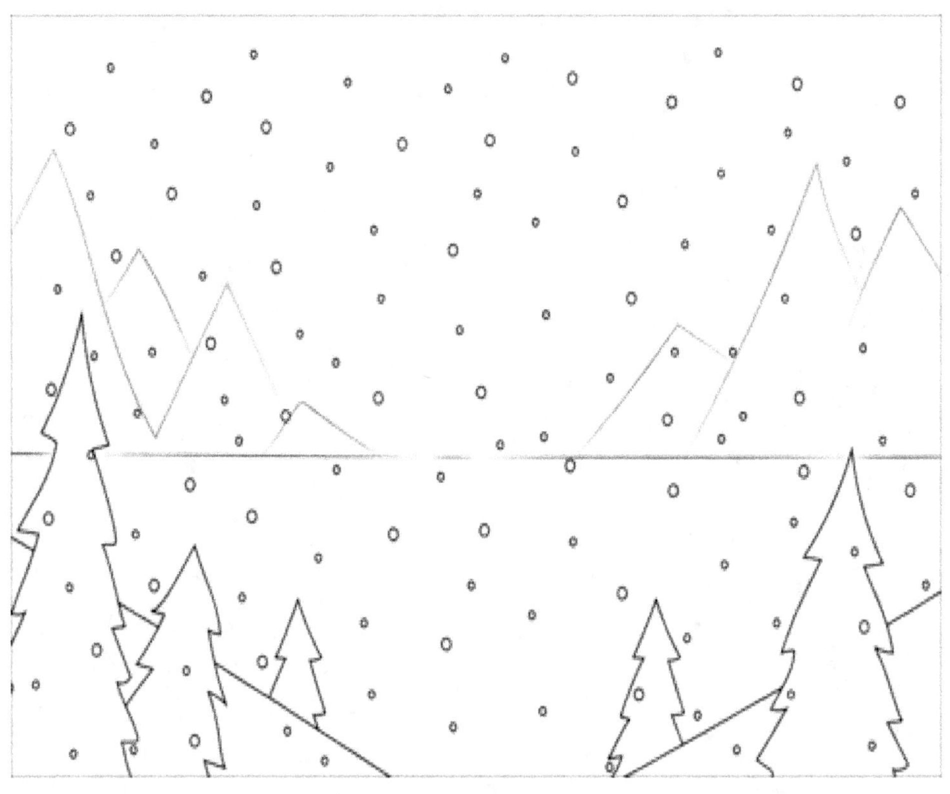

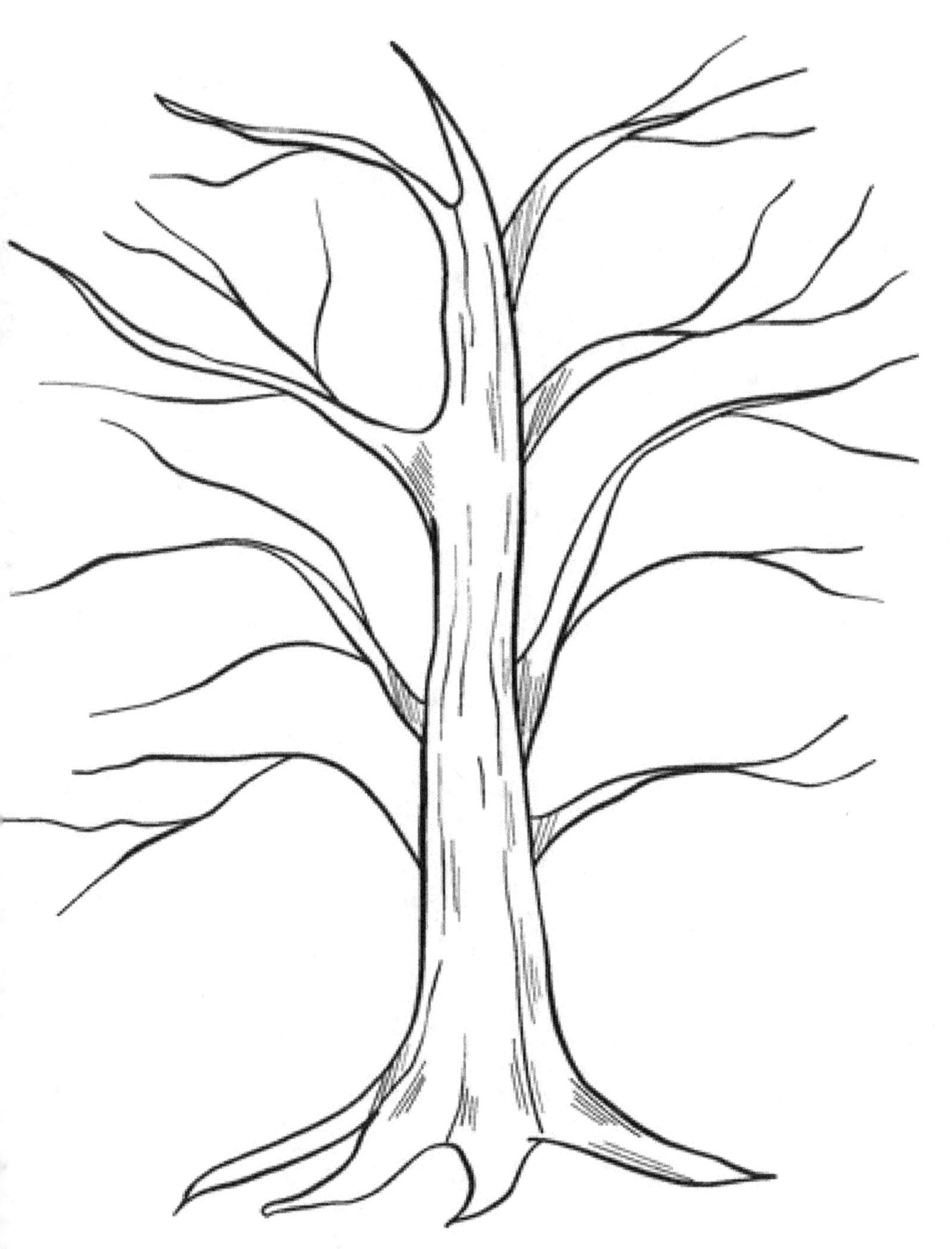

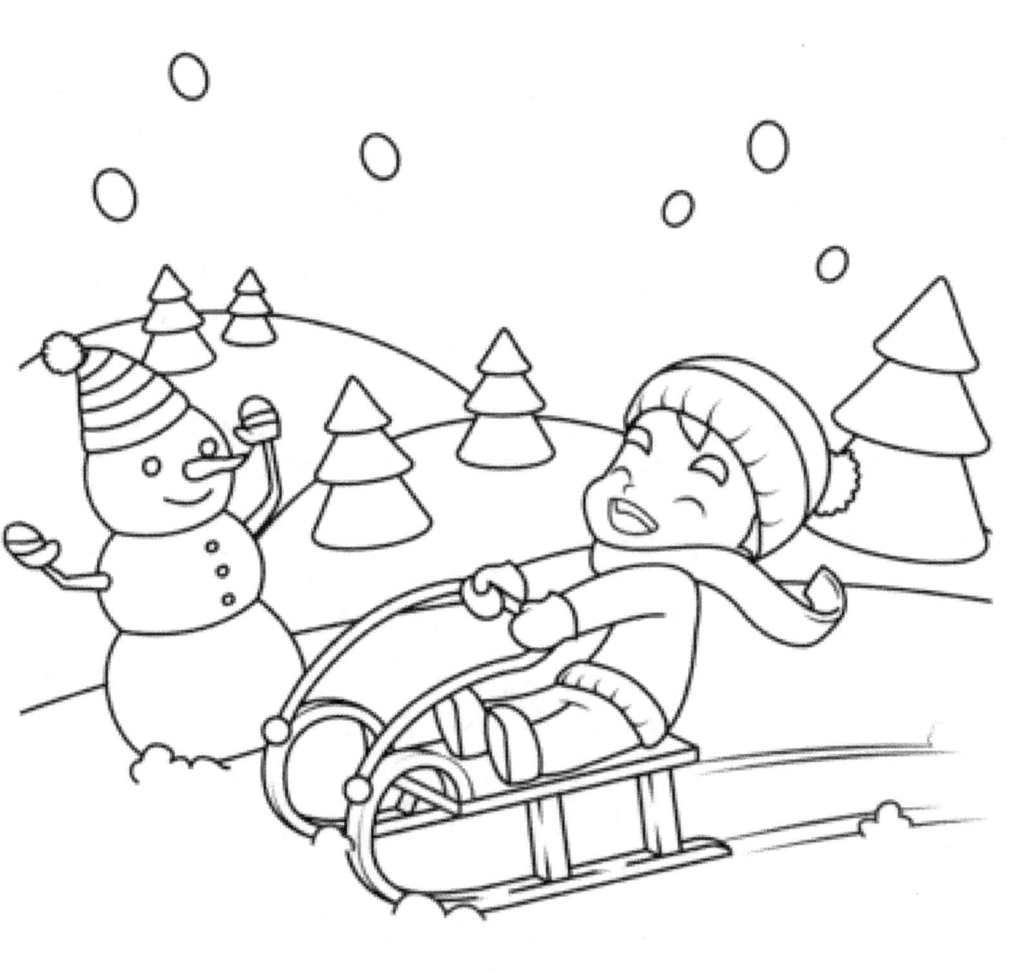

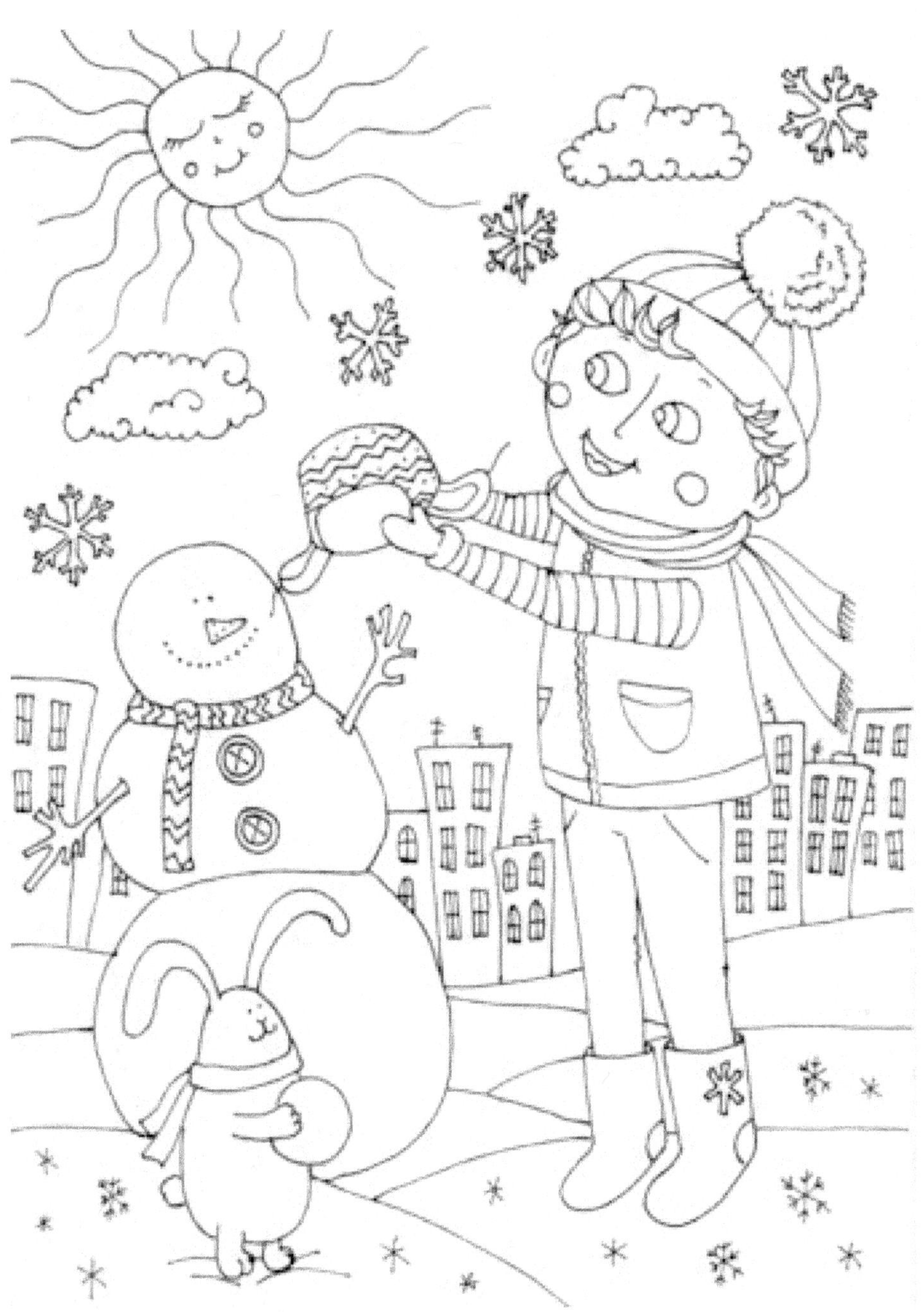

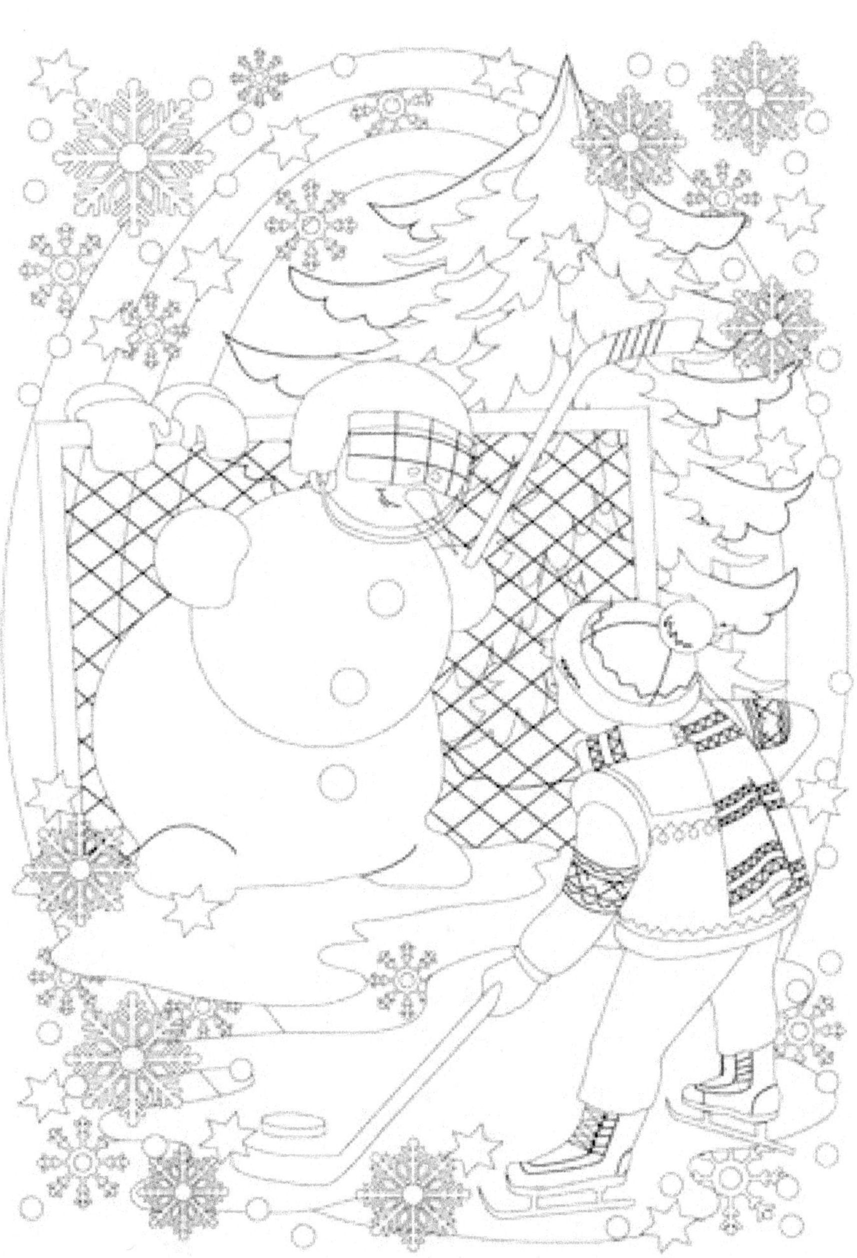

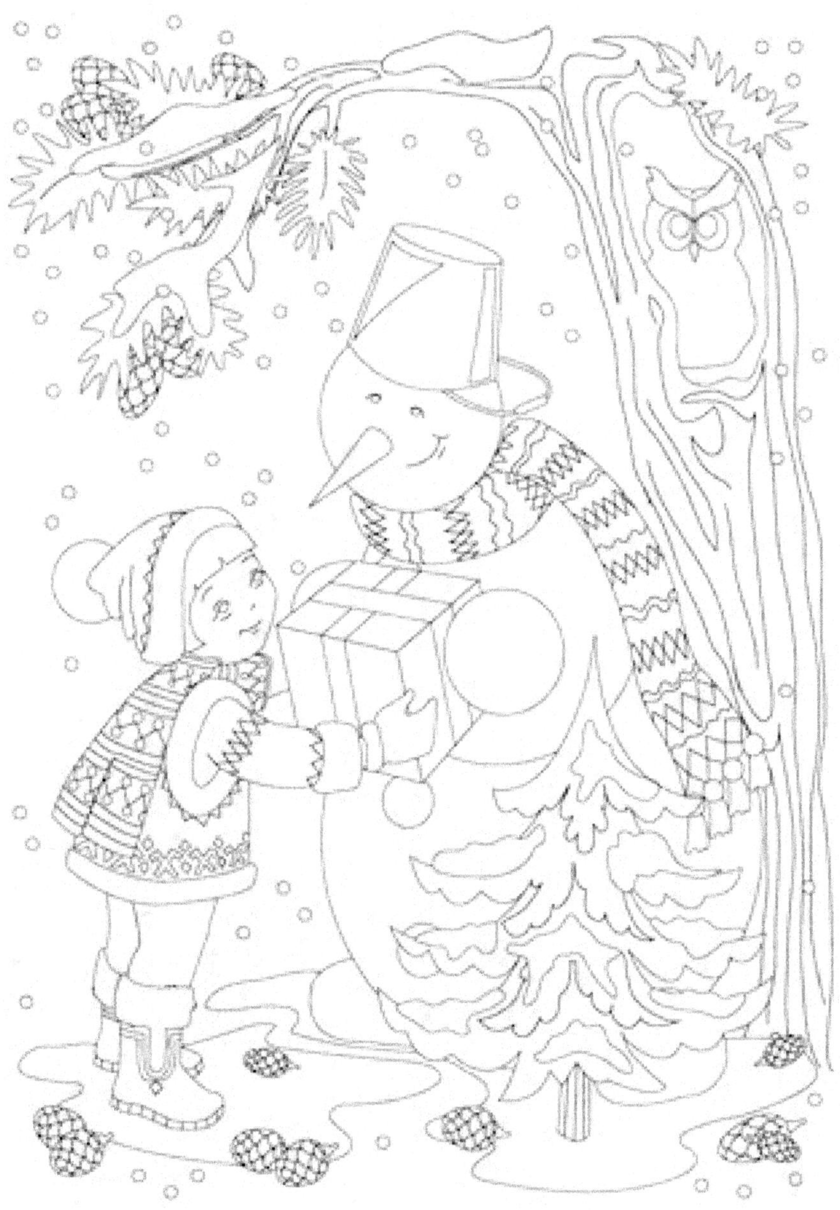

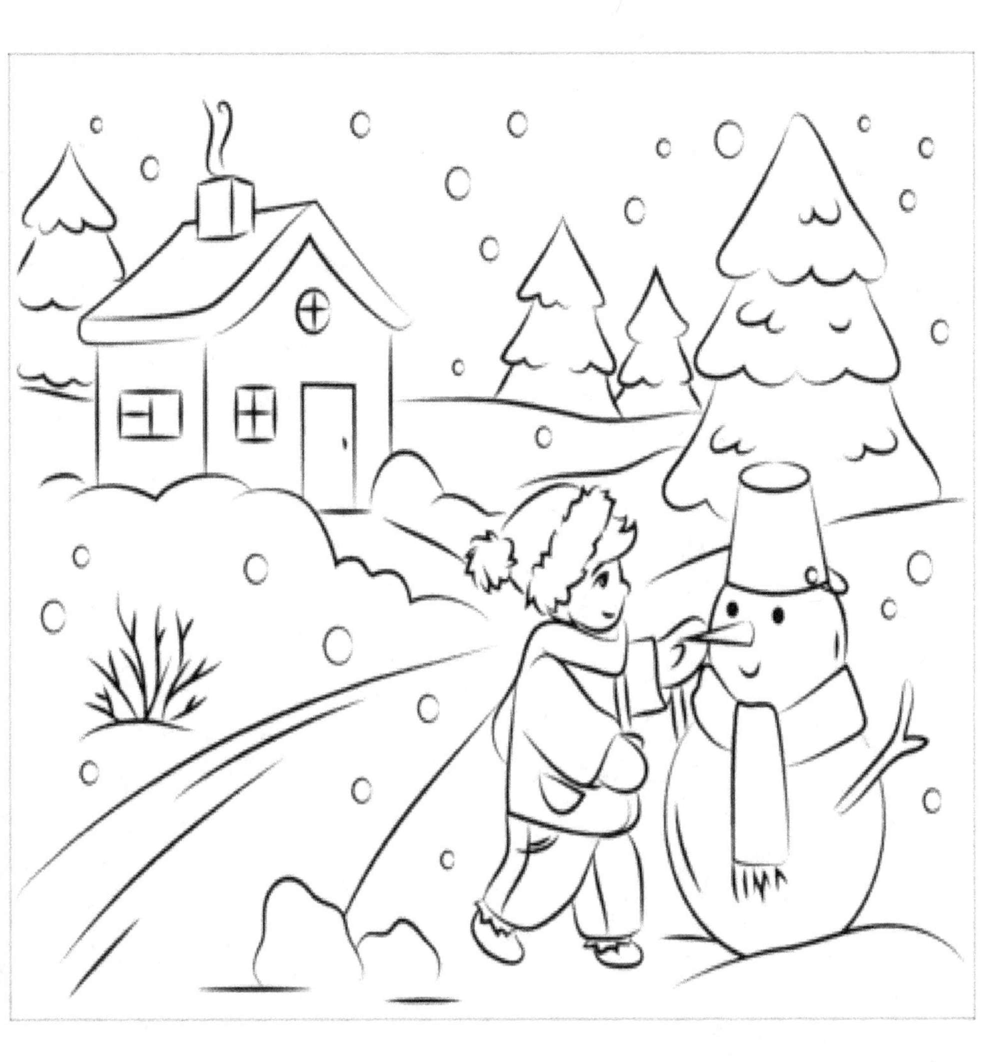

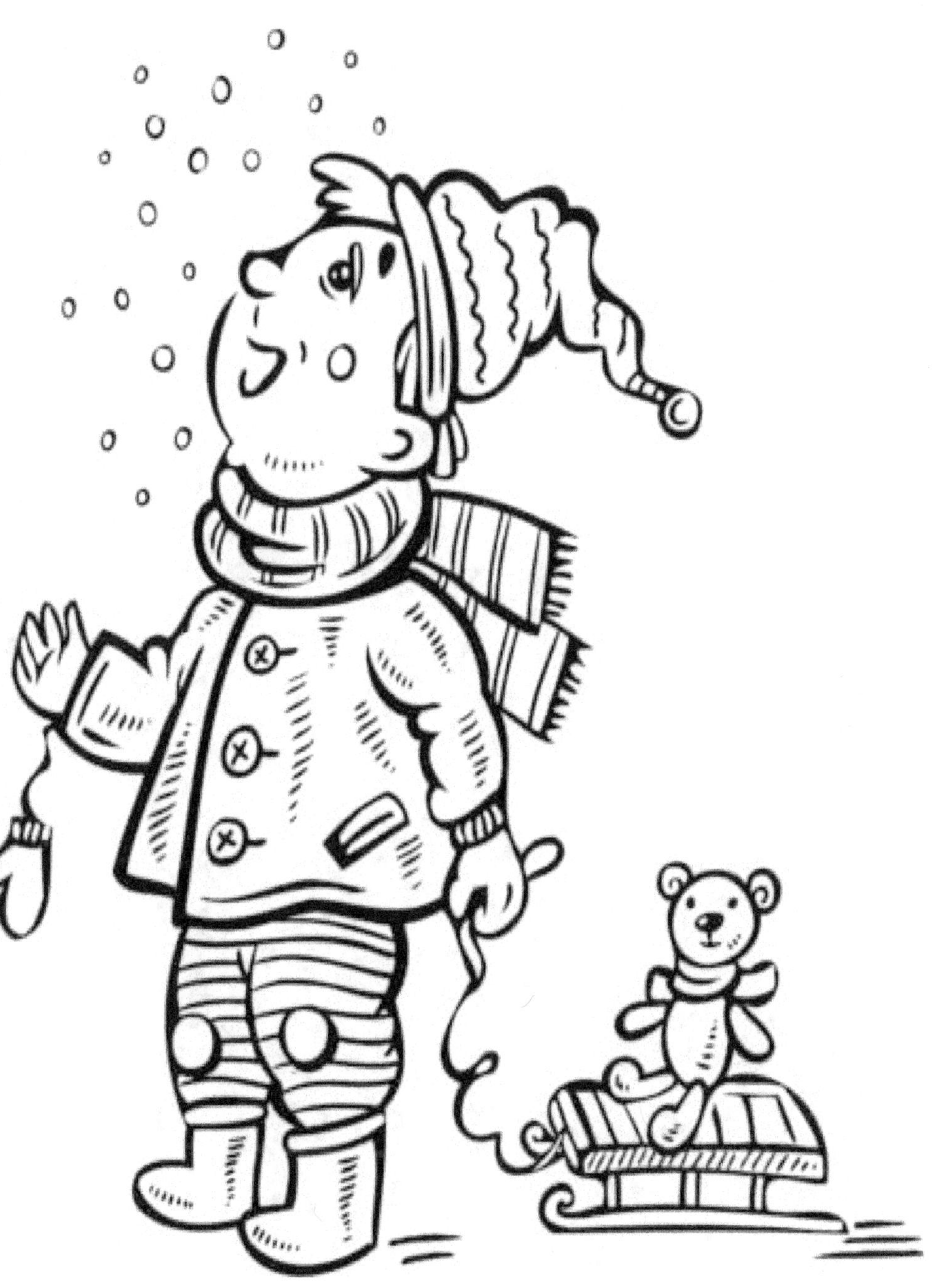

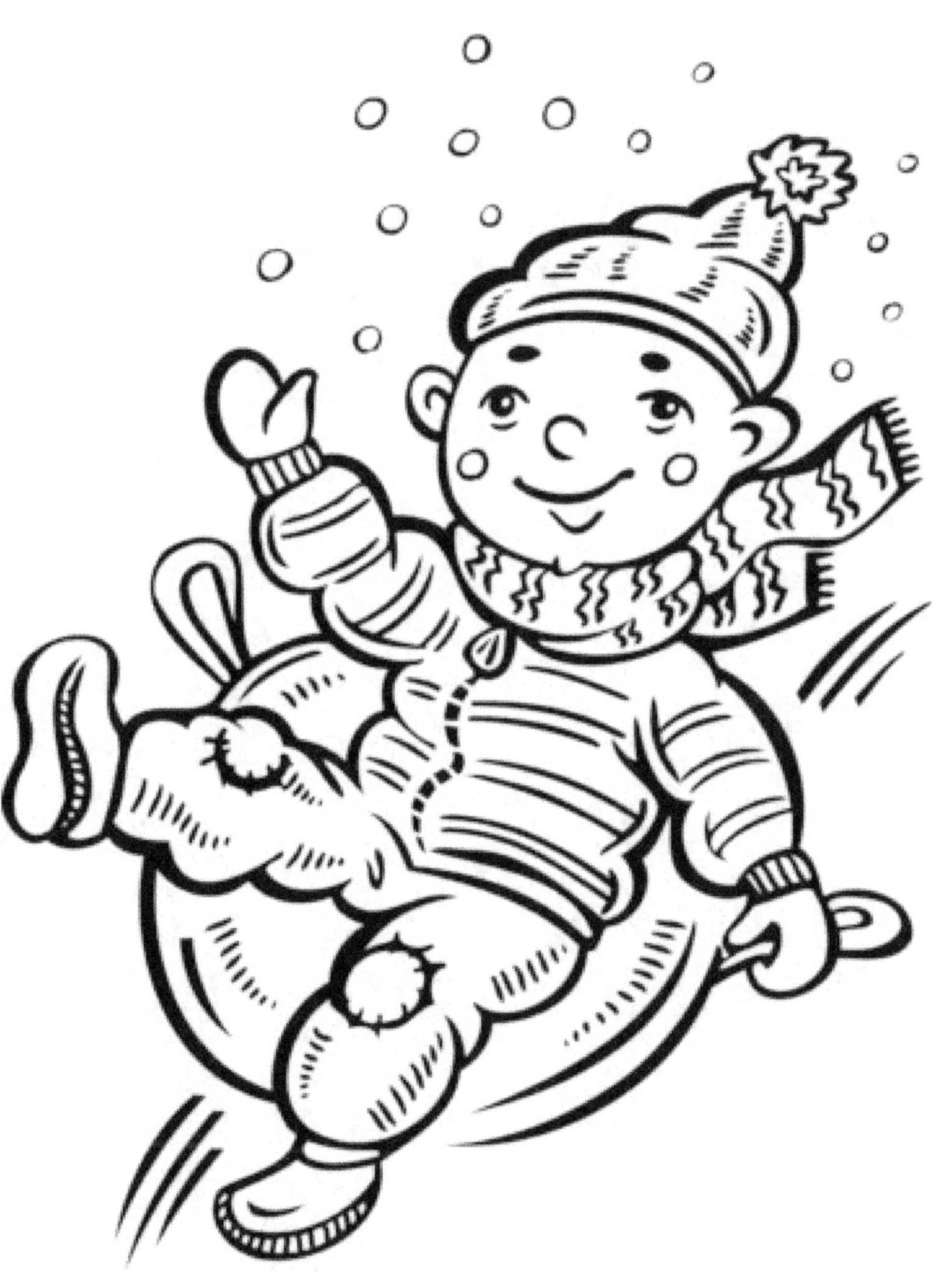

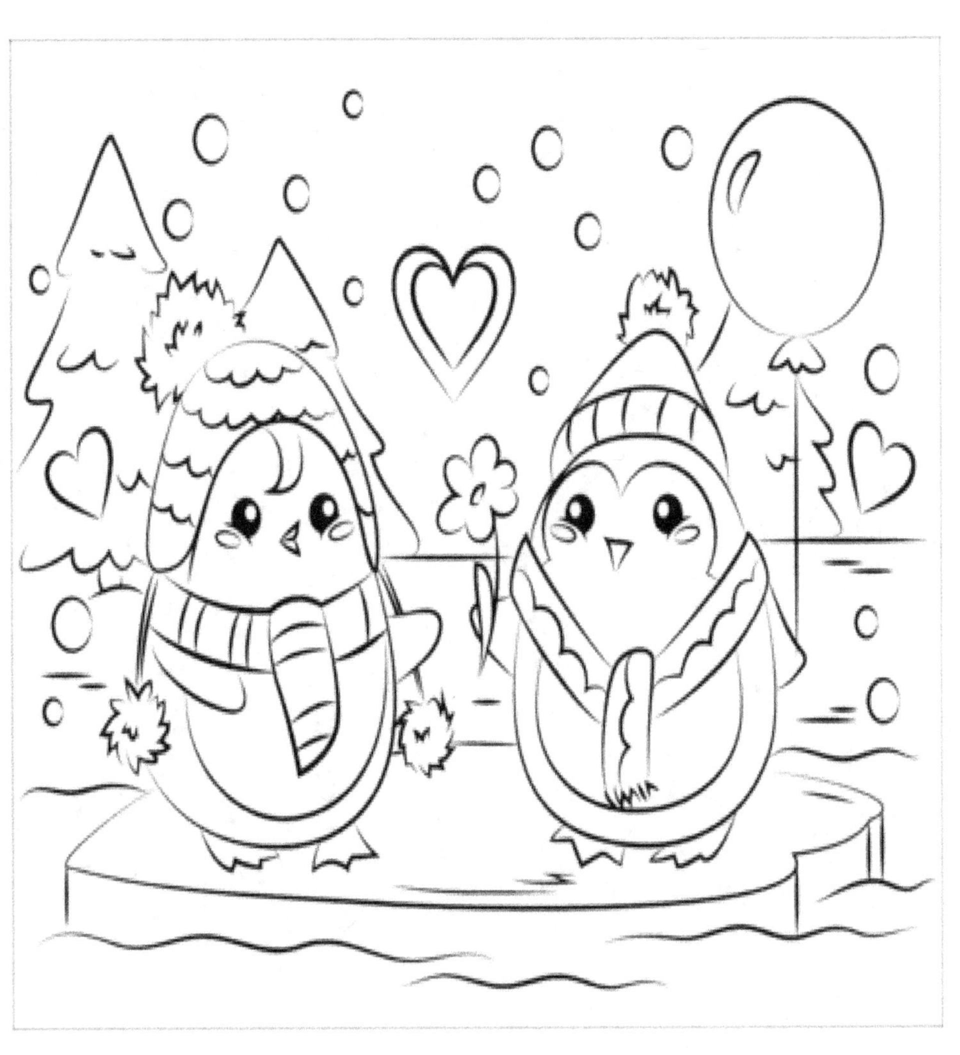

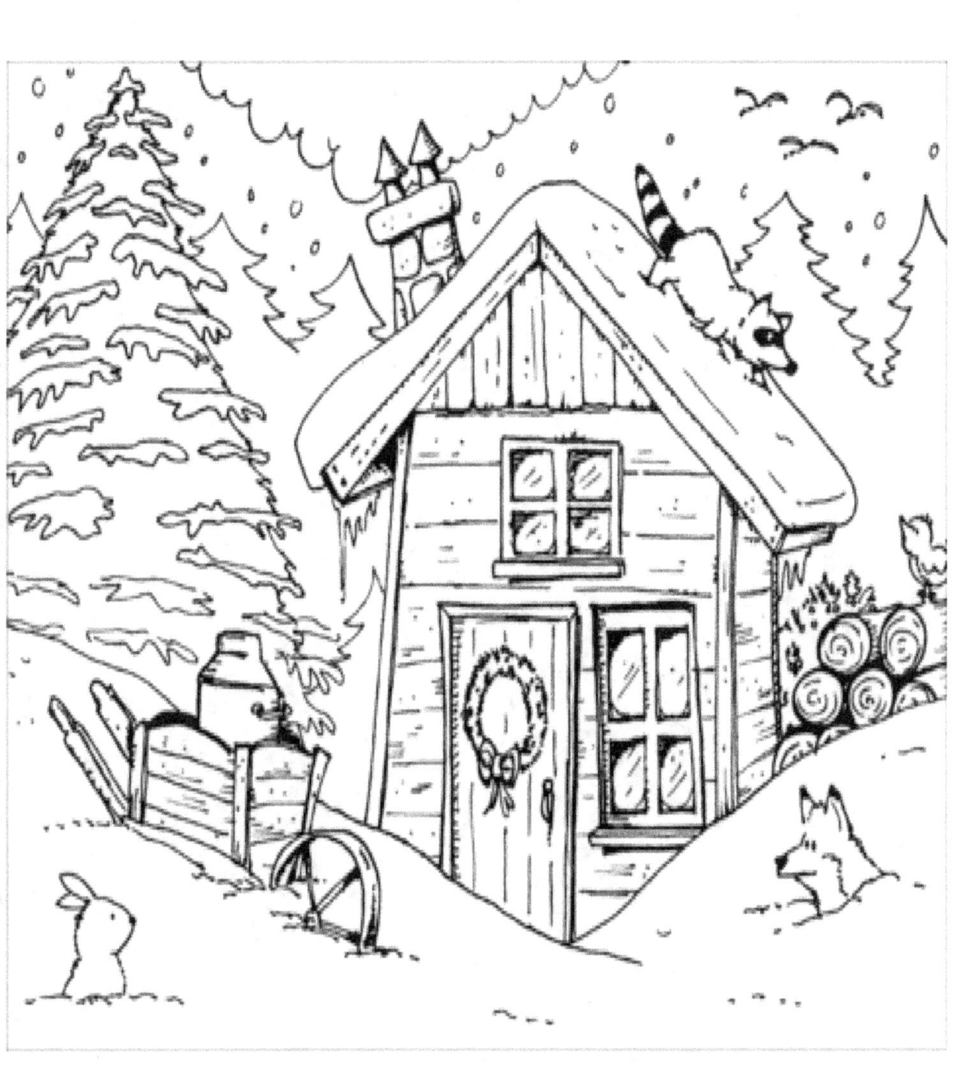

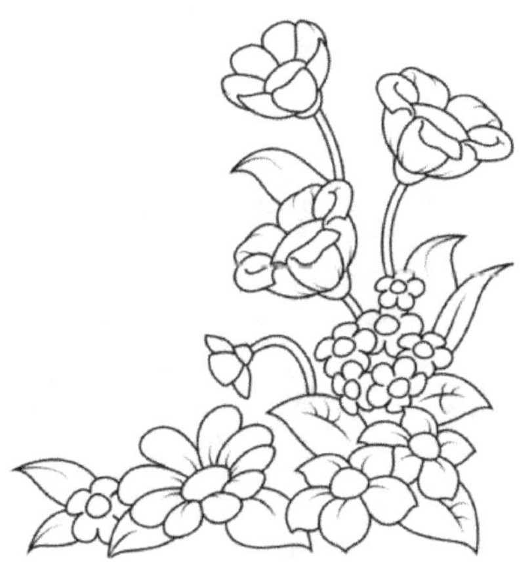

Spring

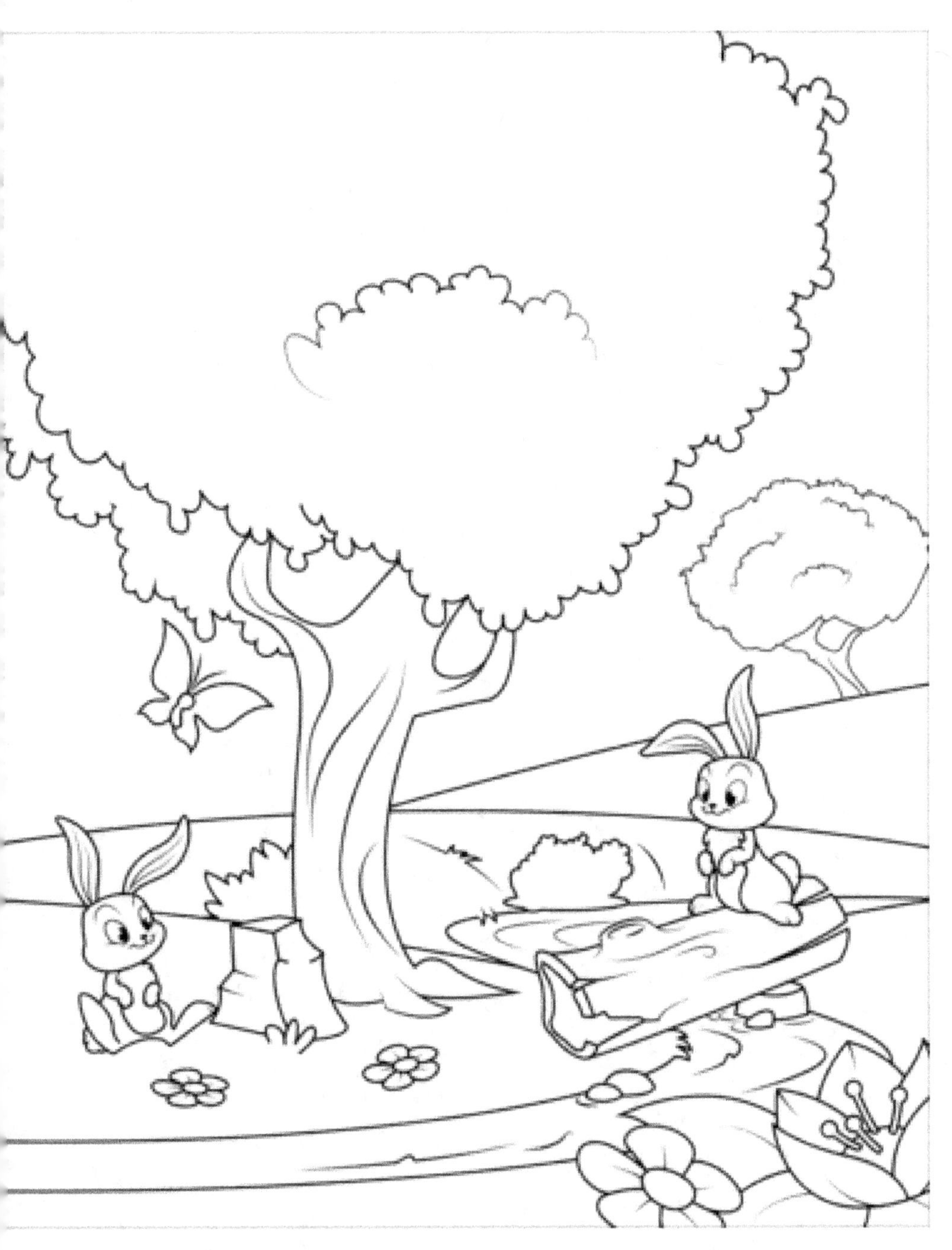

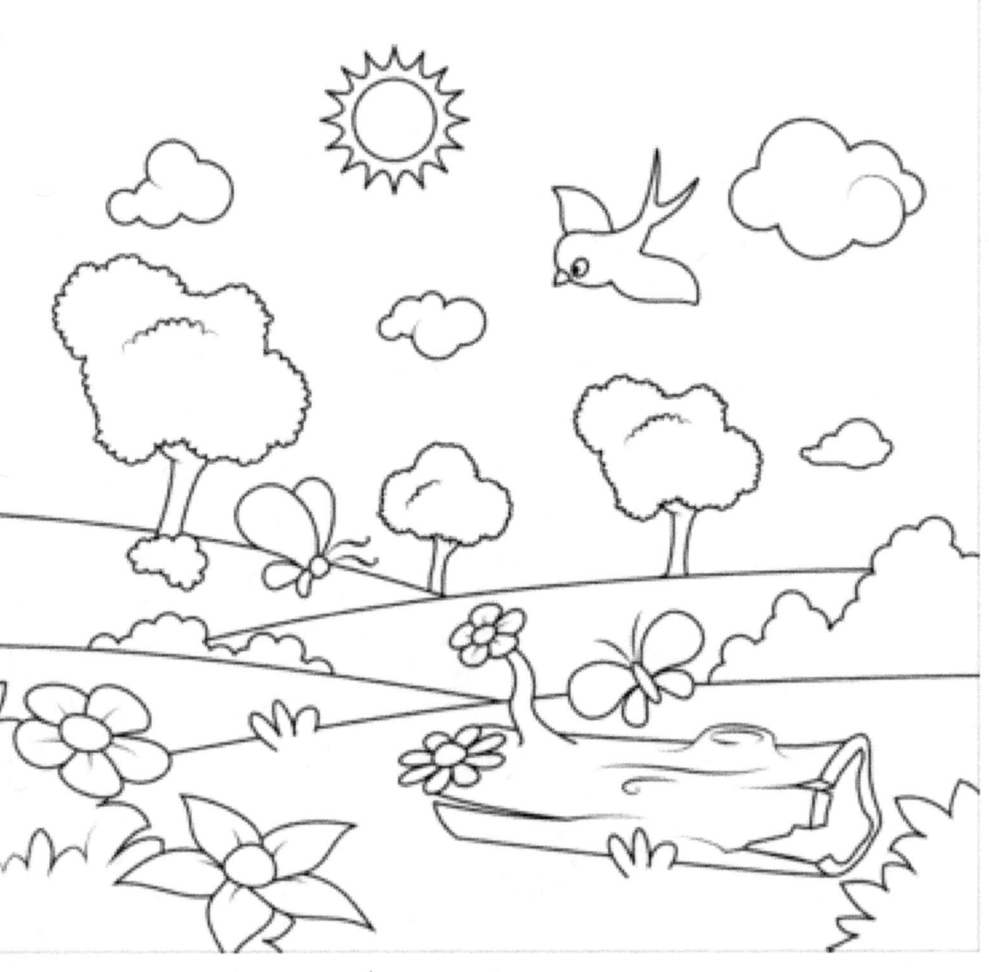

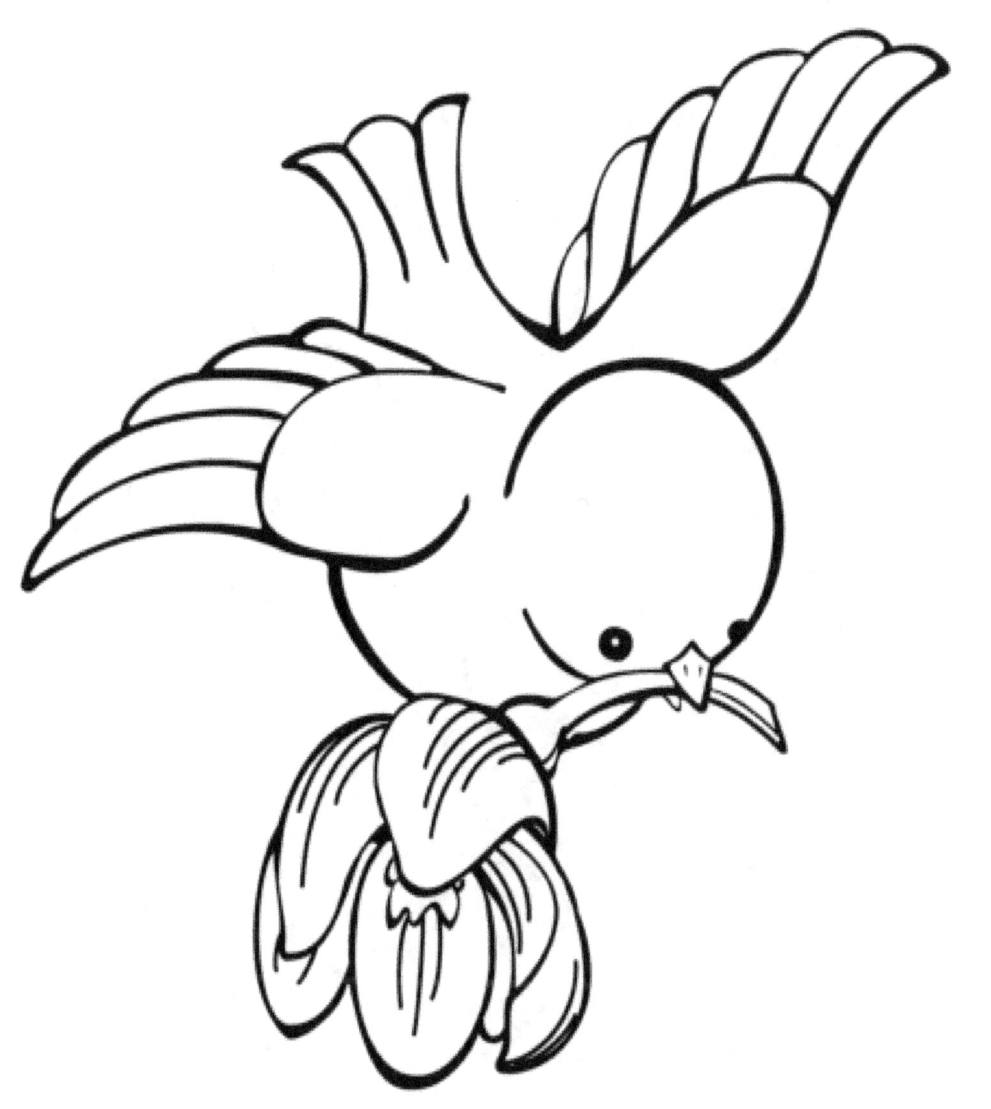

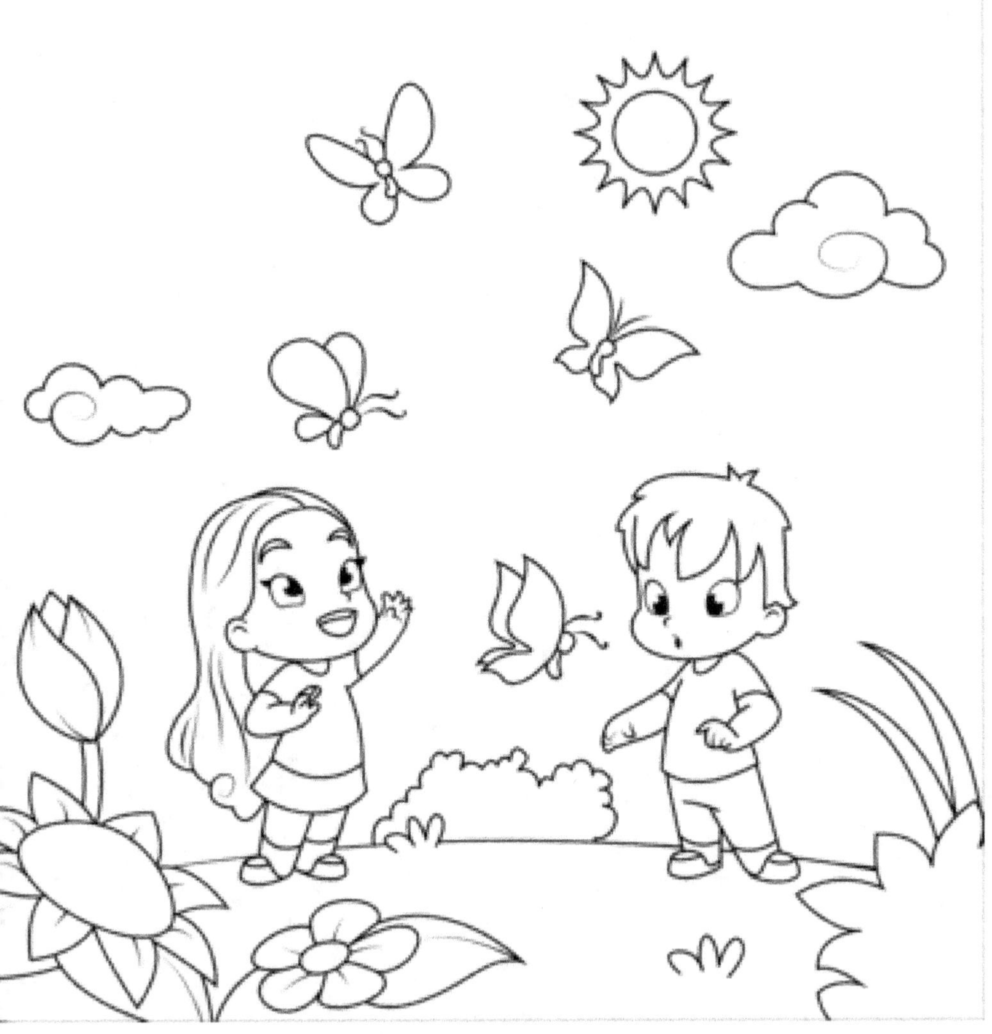

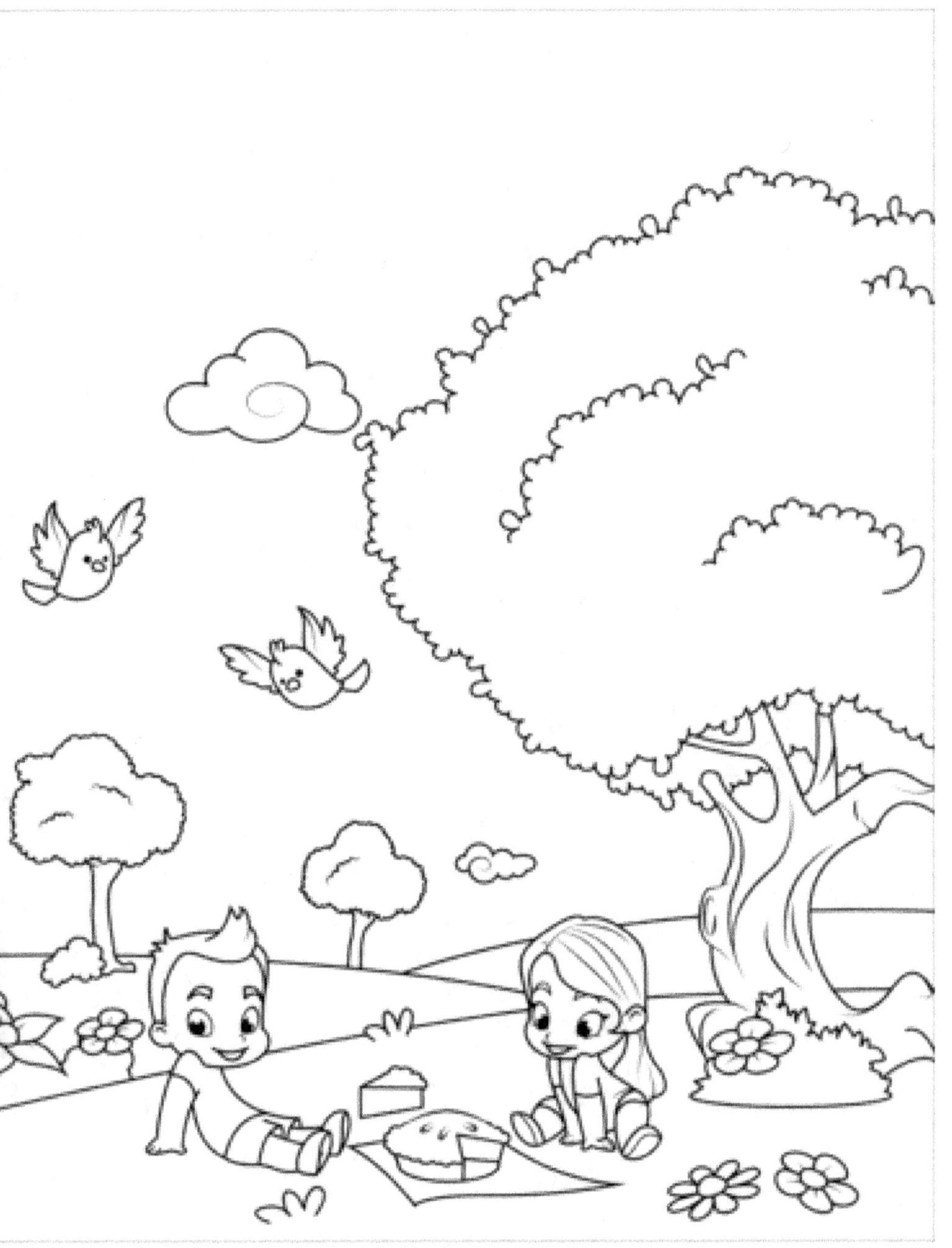

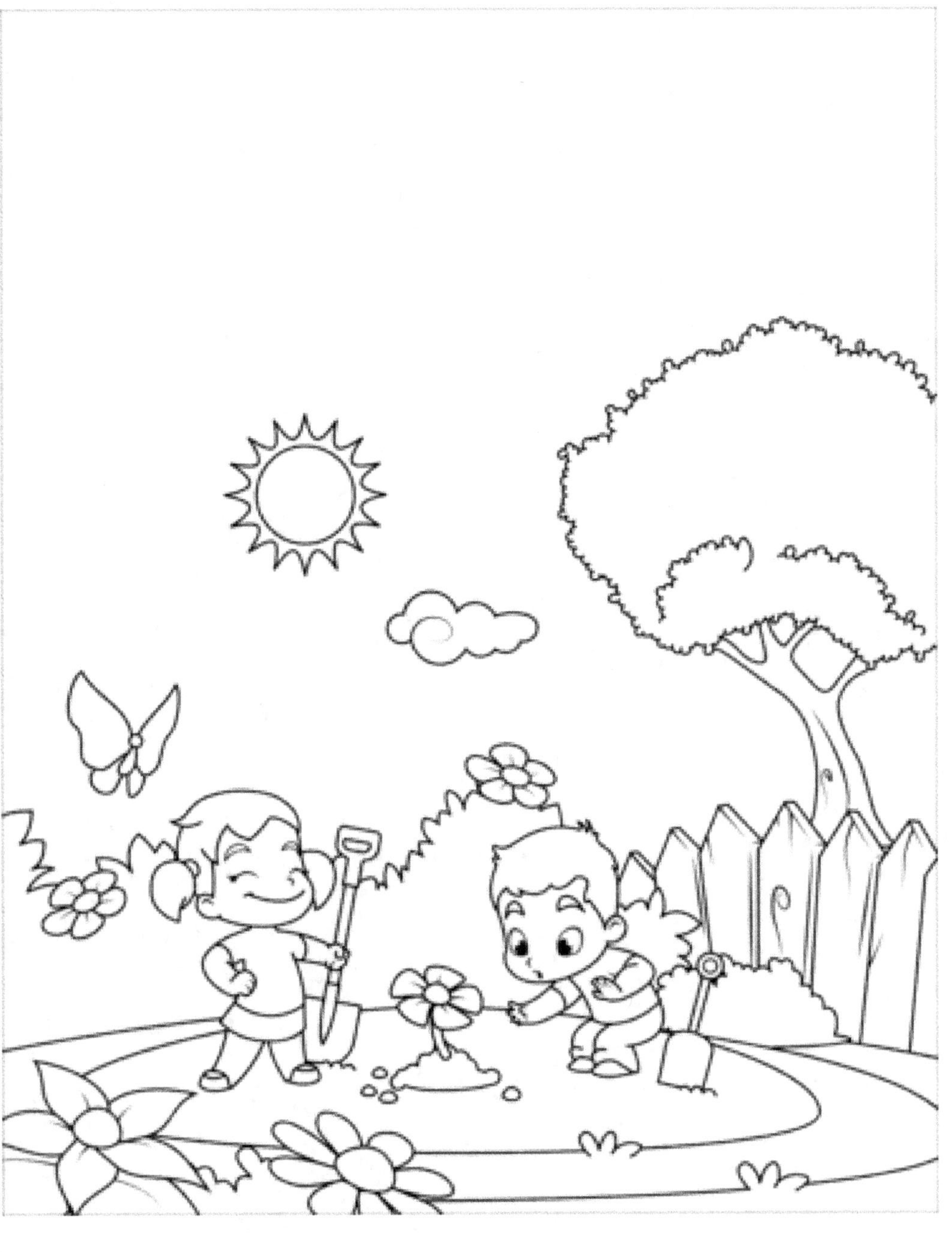

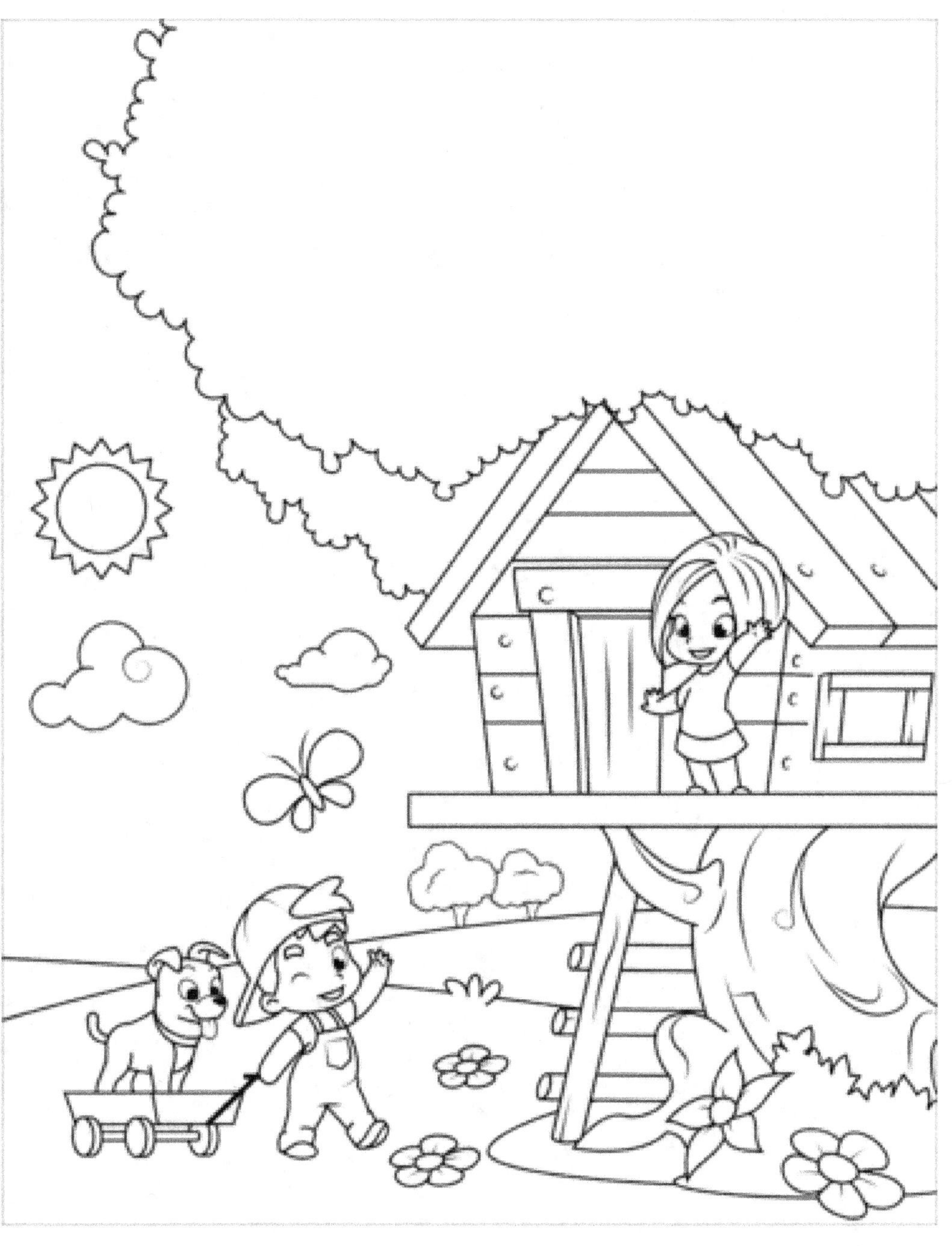

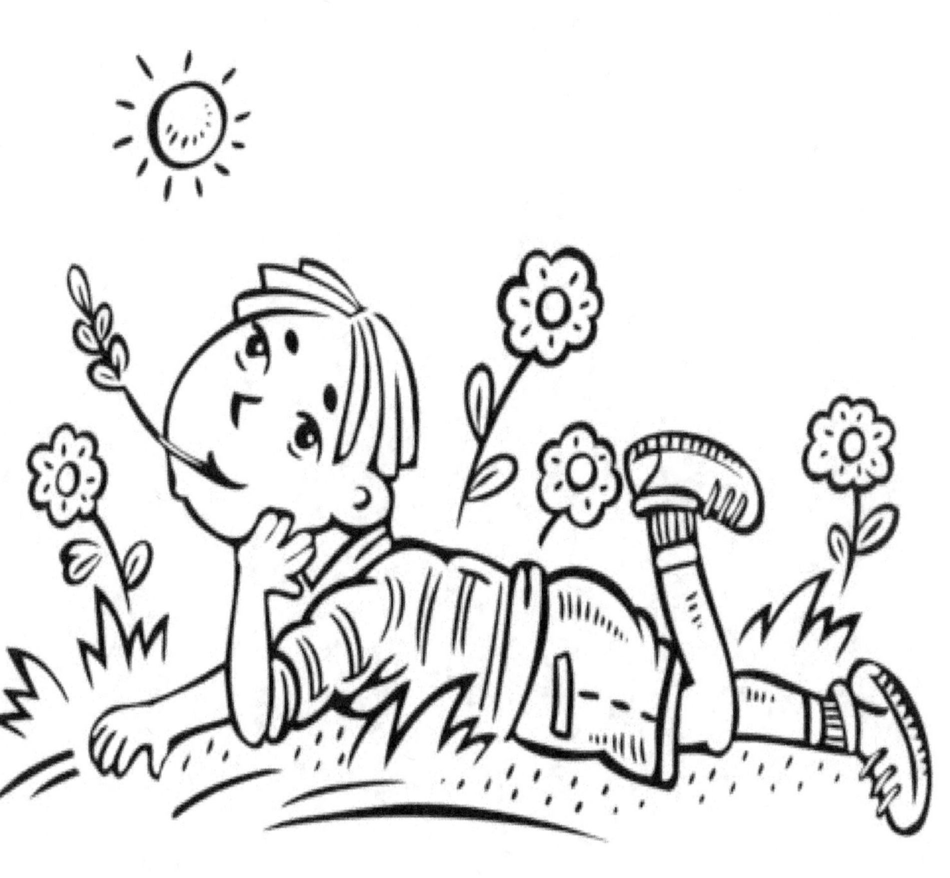

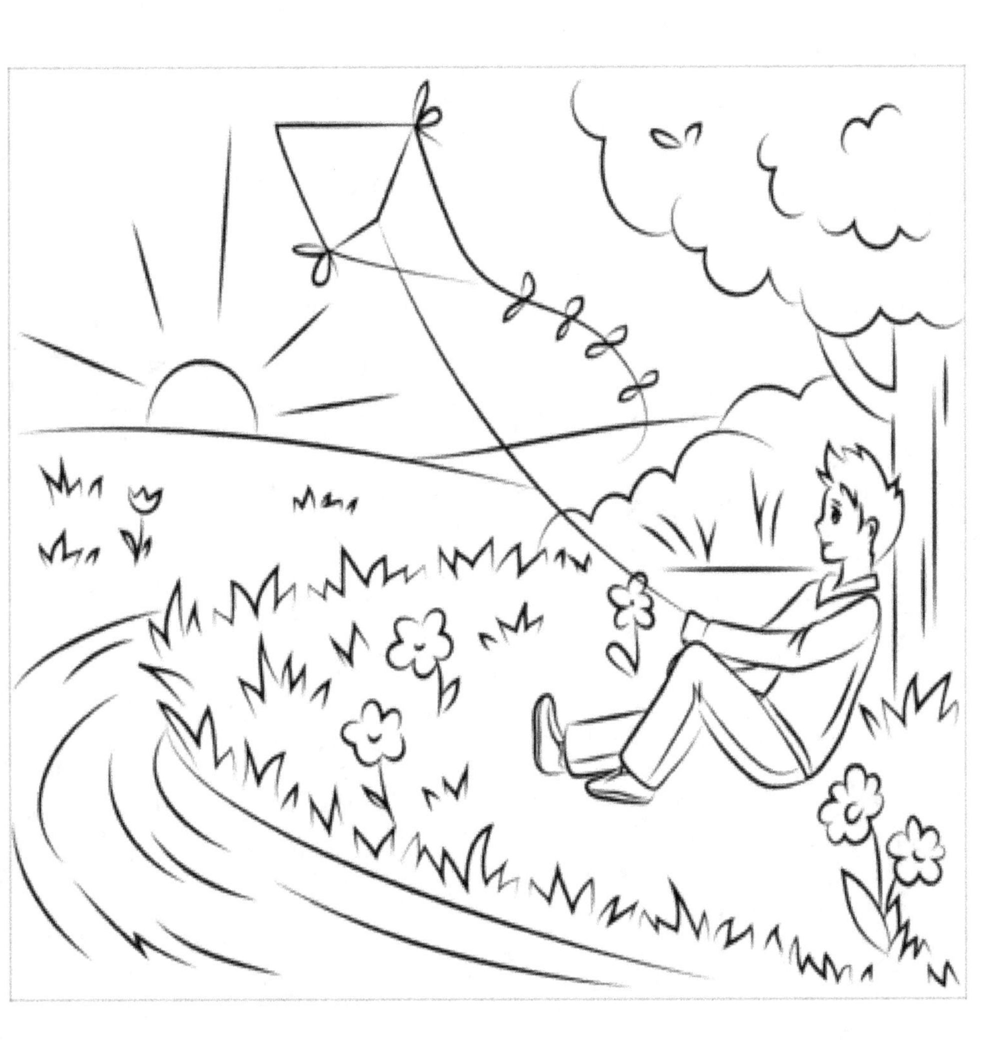

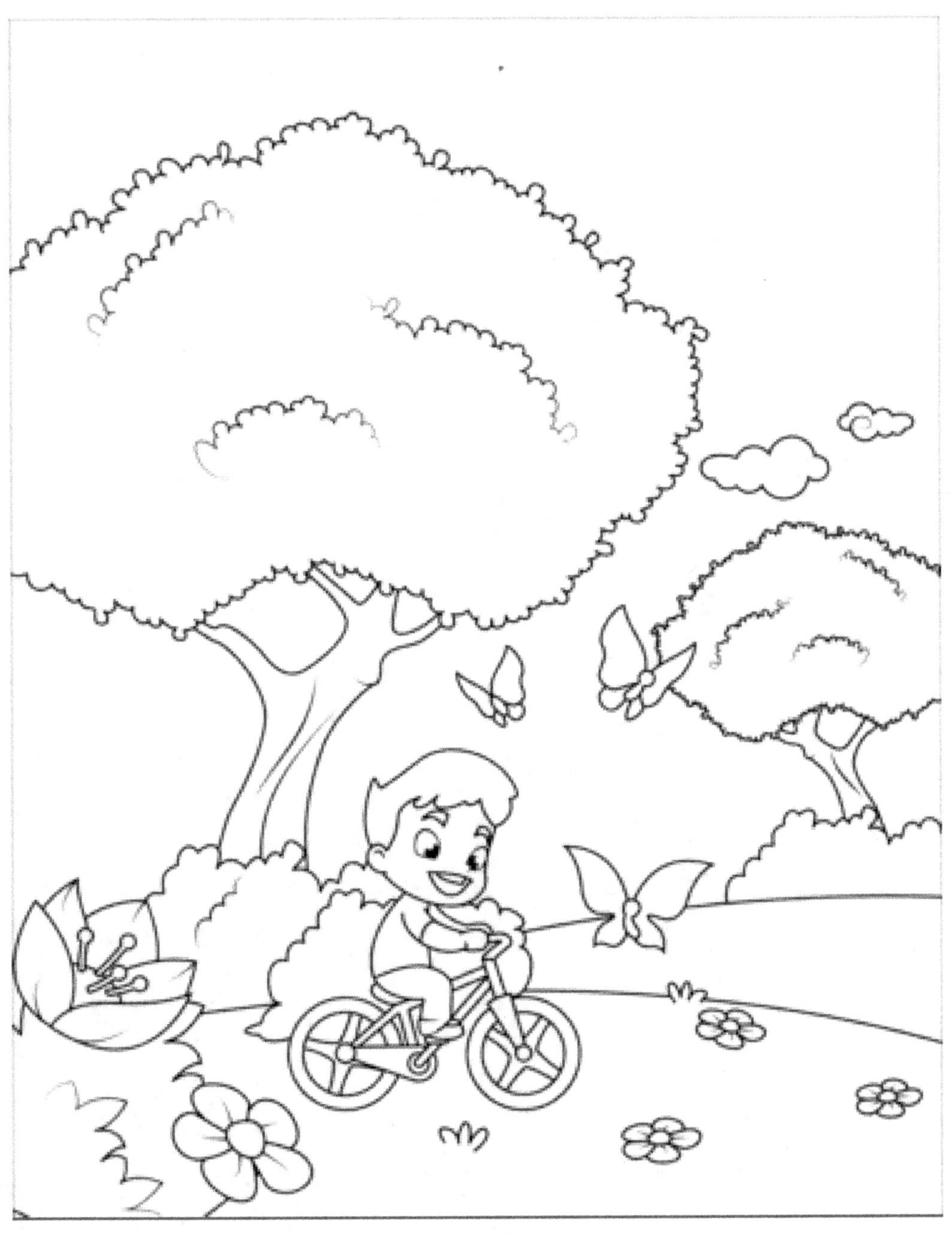

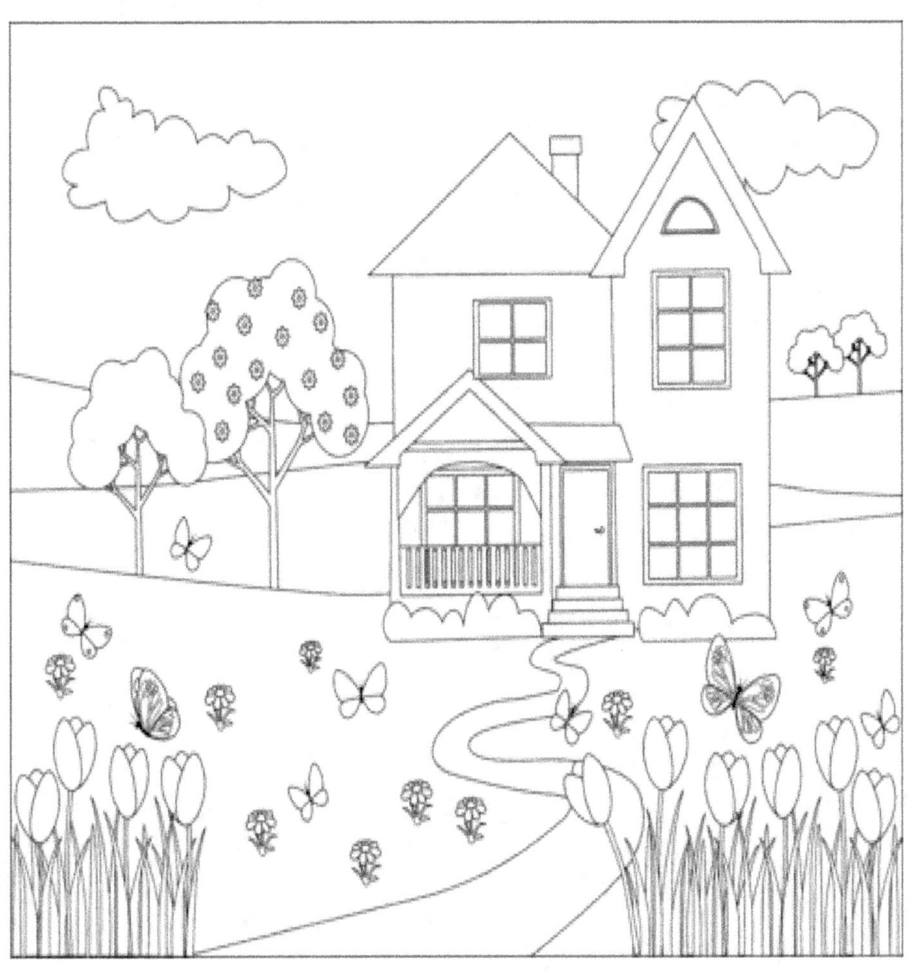

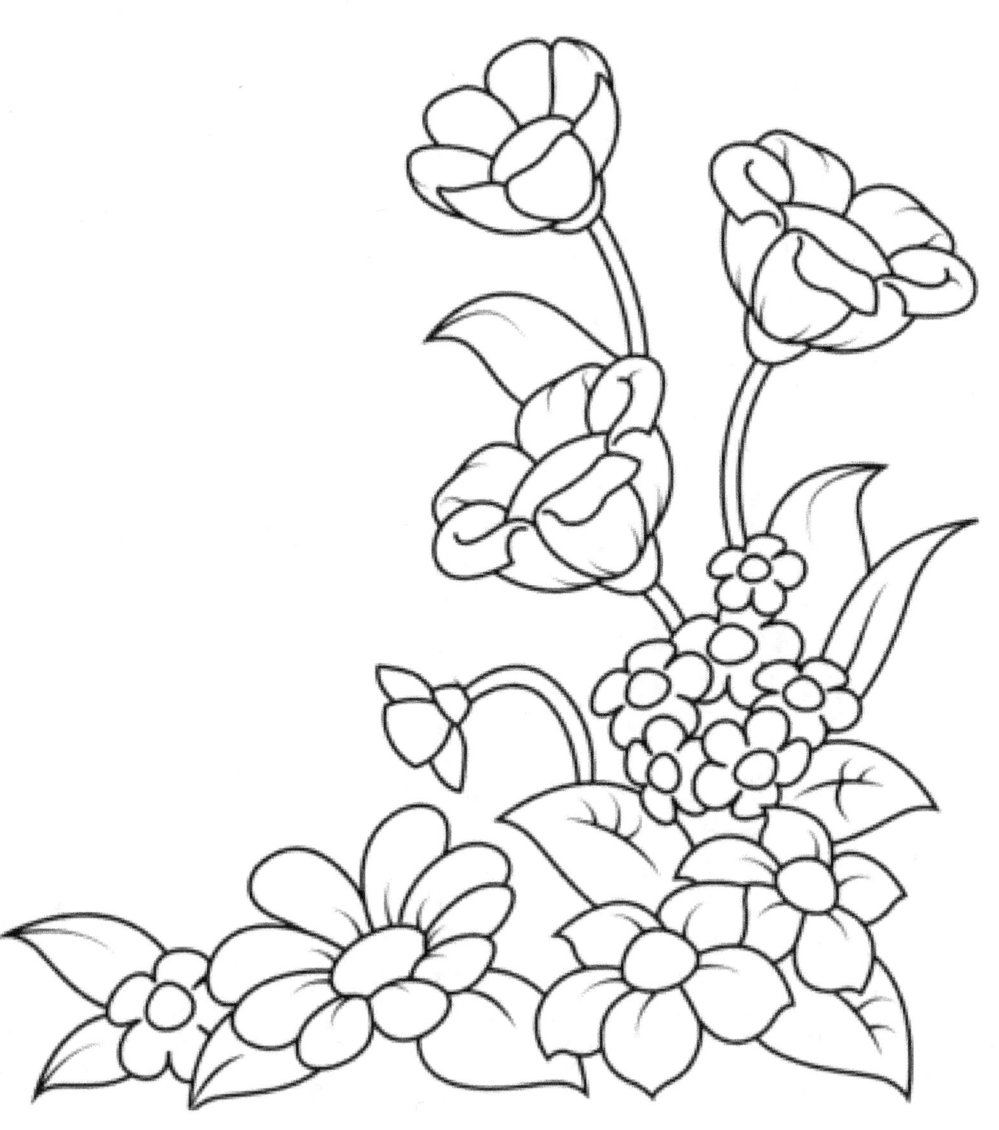

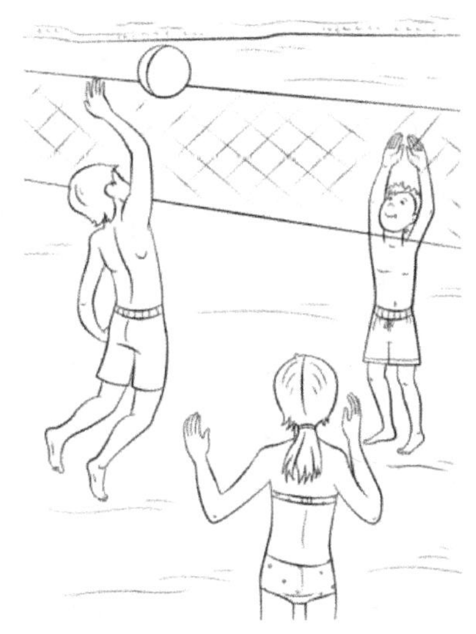

Summer

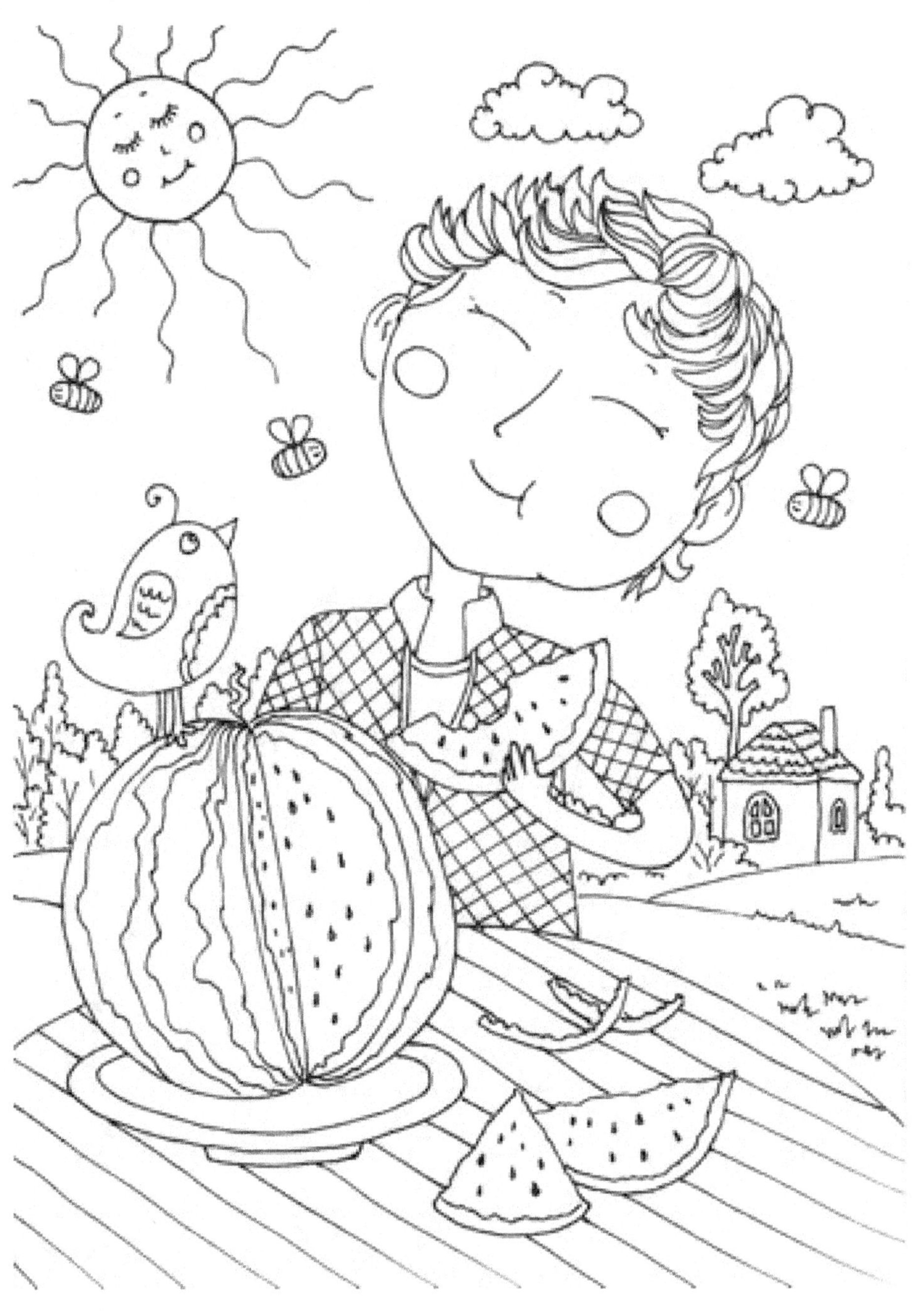

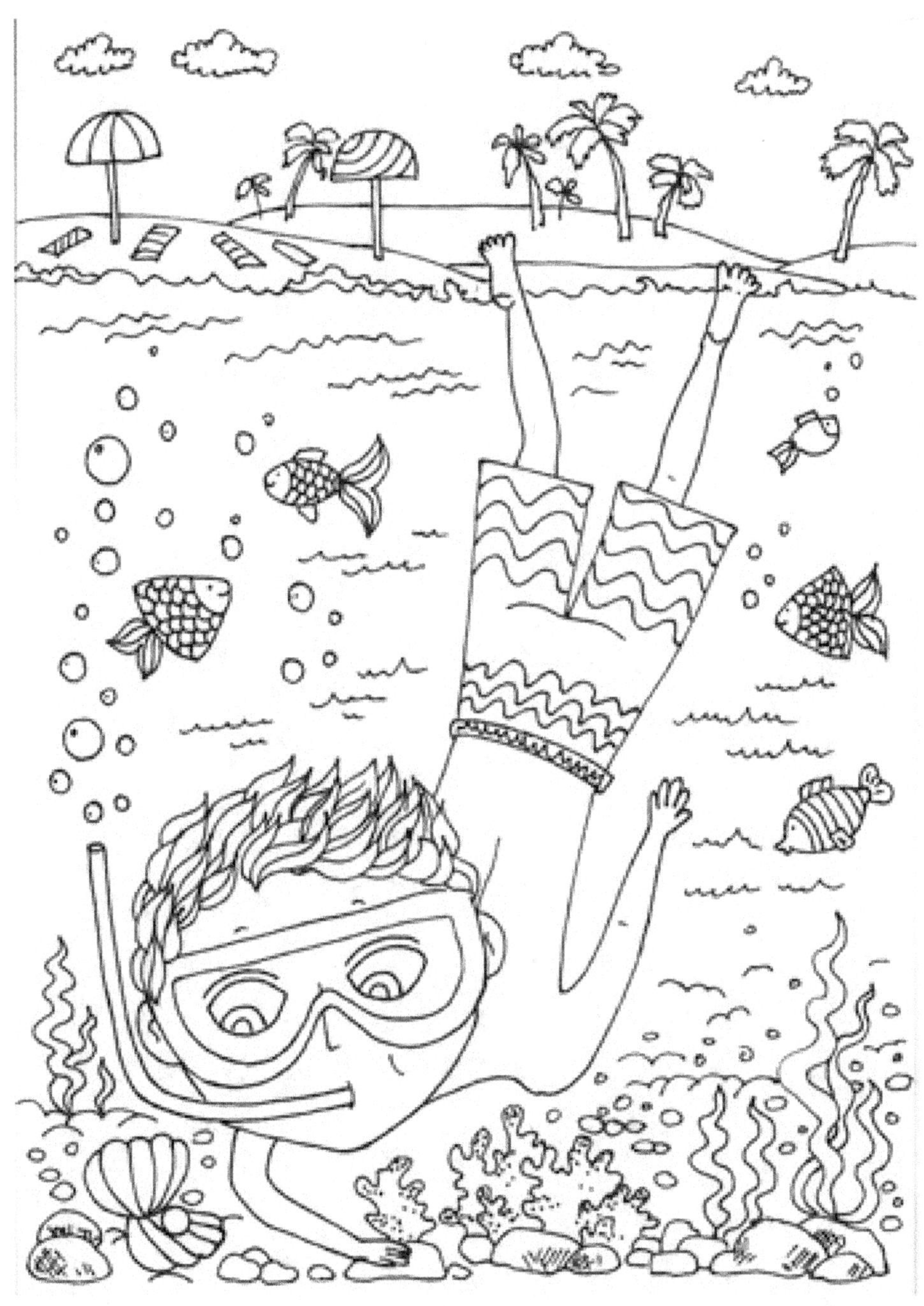

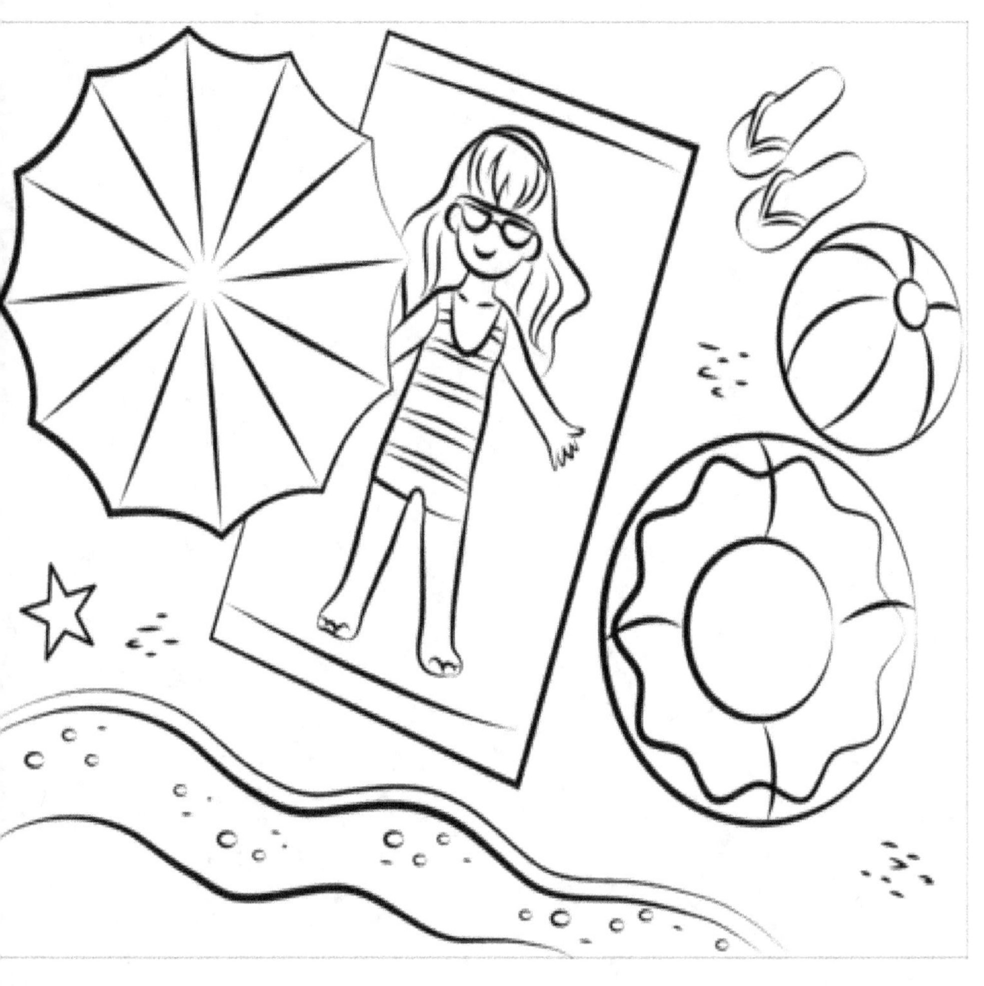

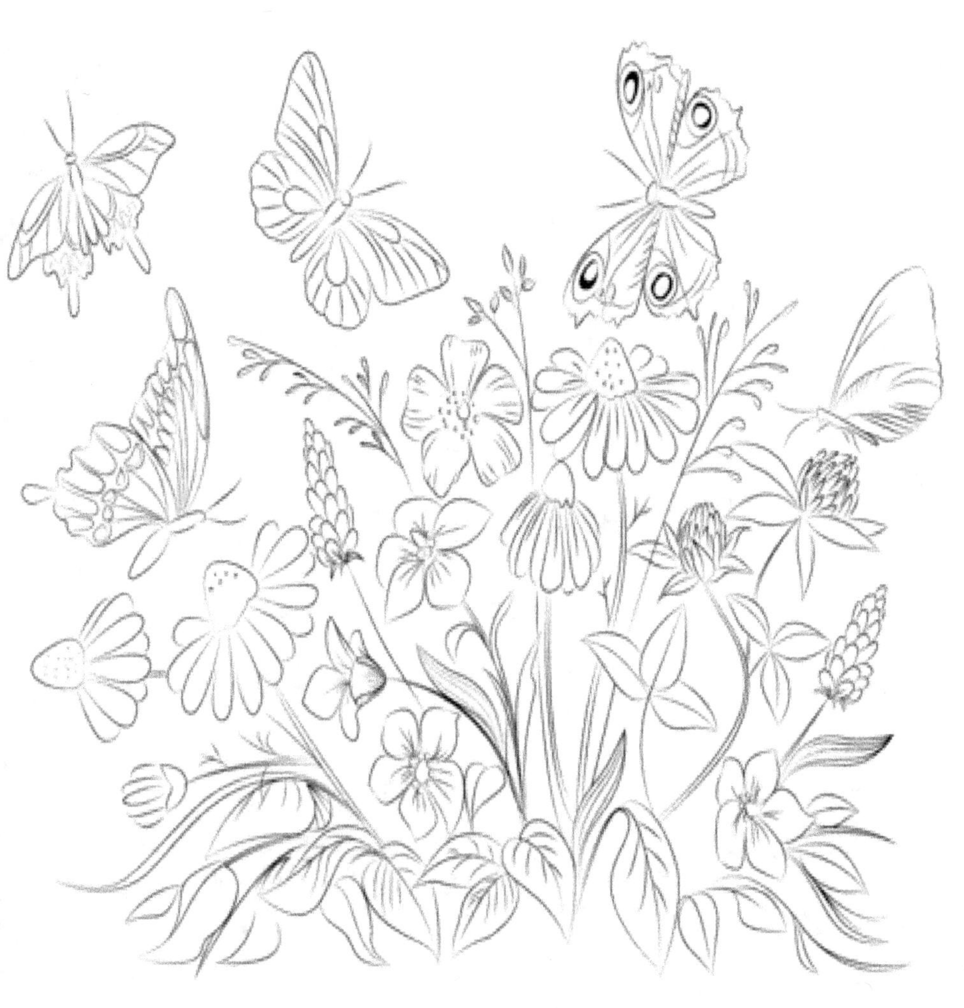

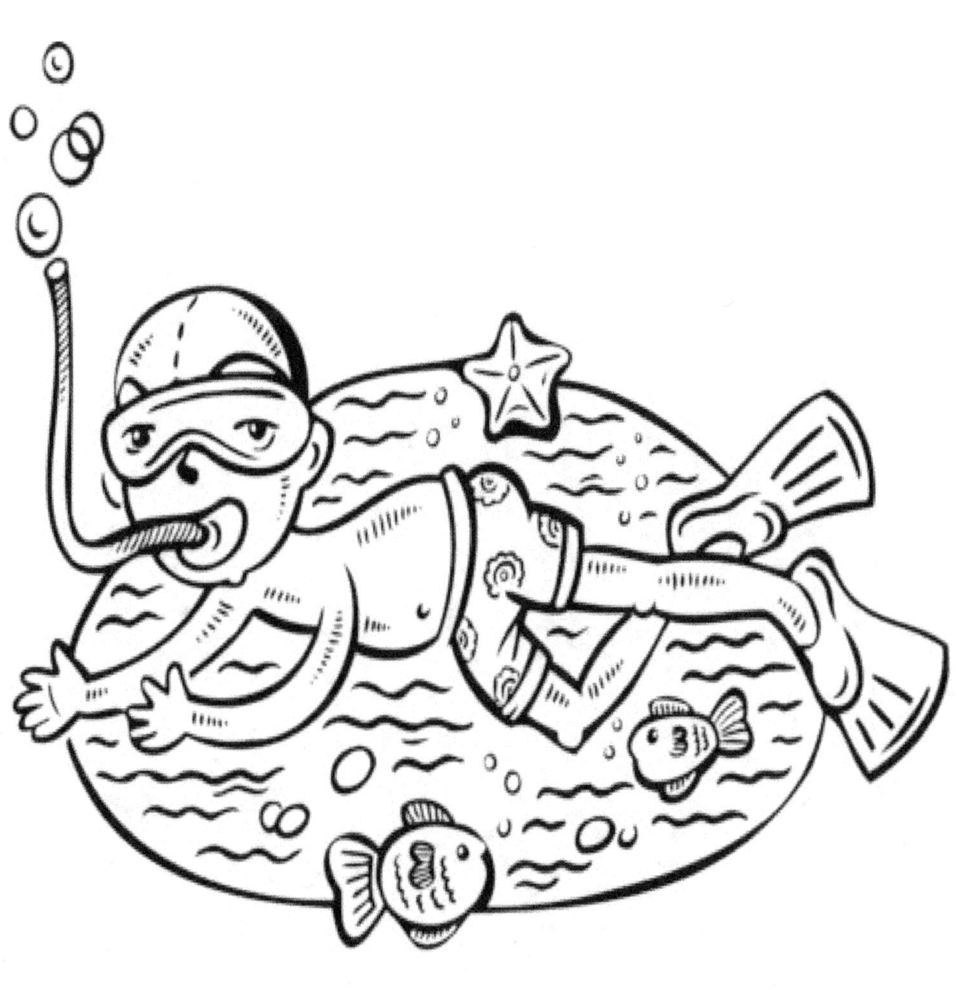

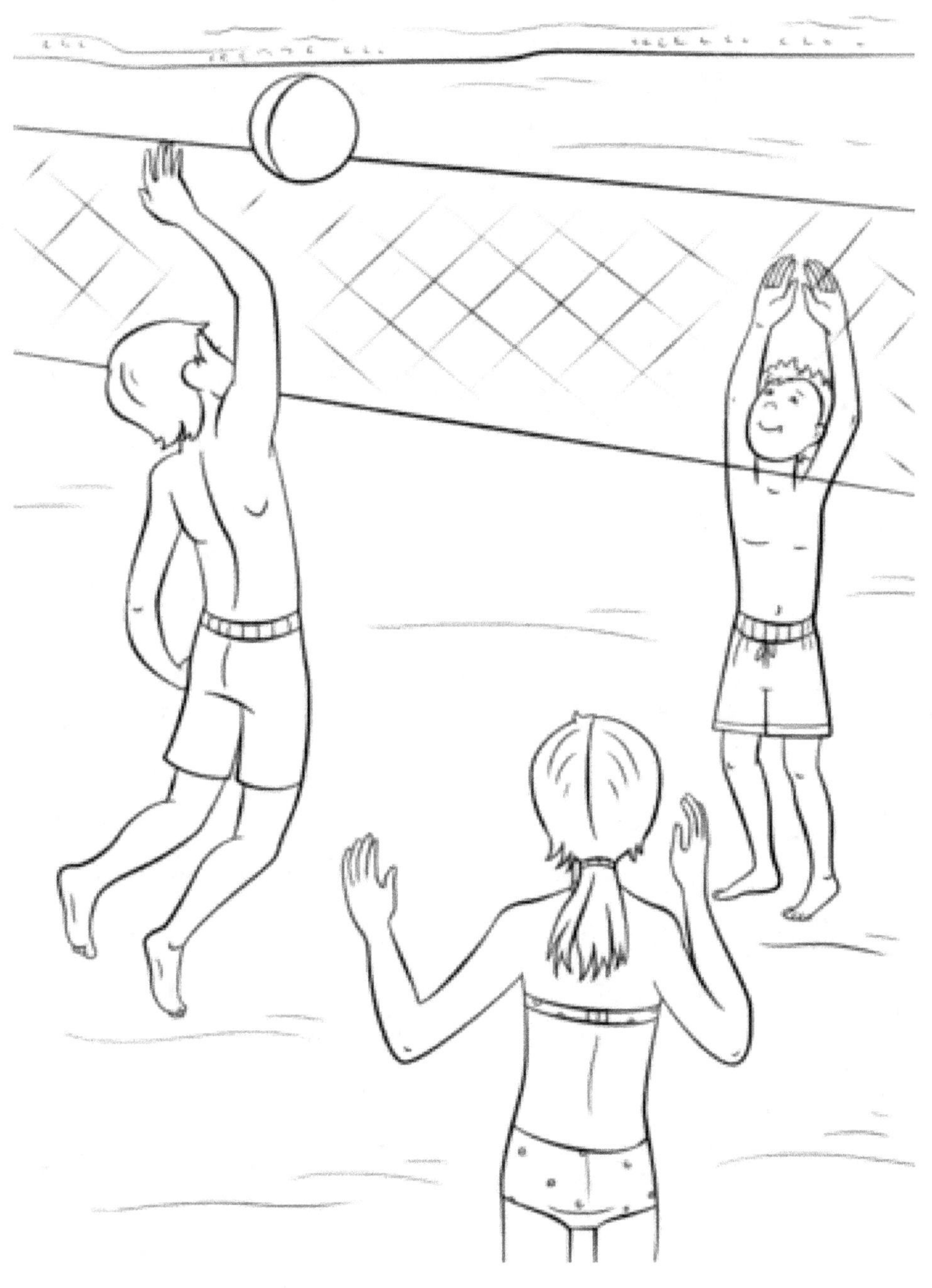

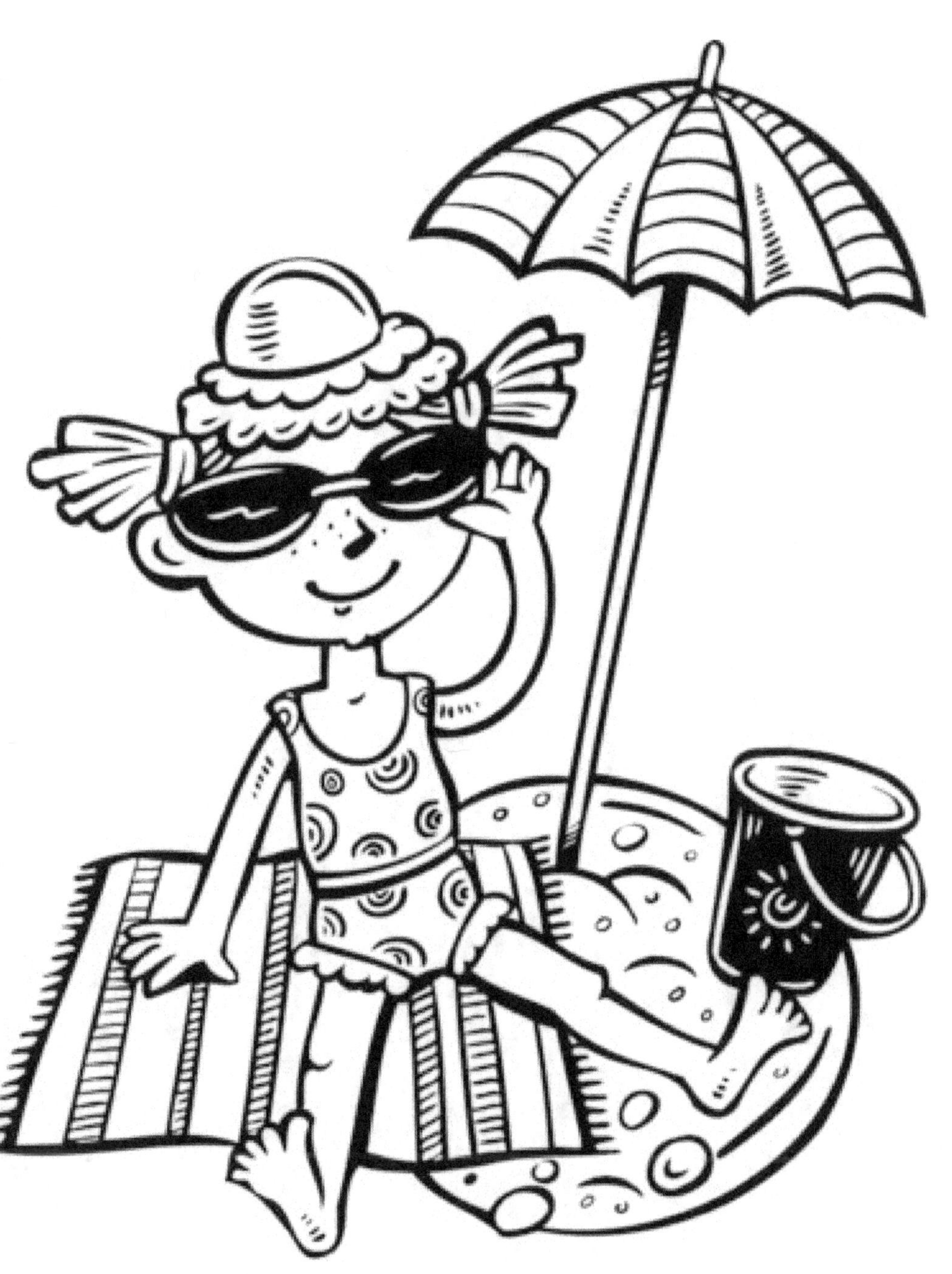

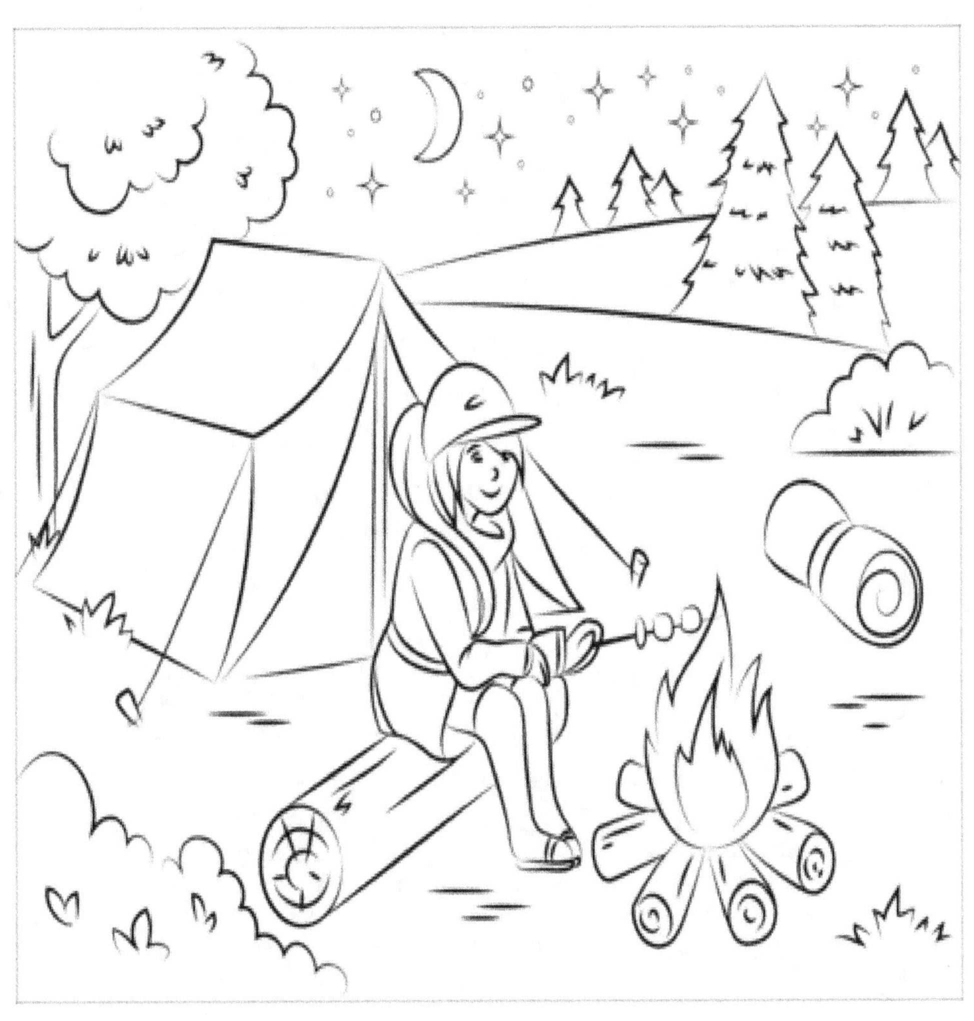

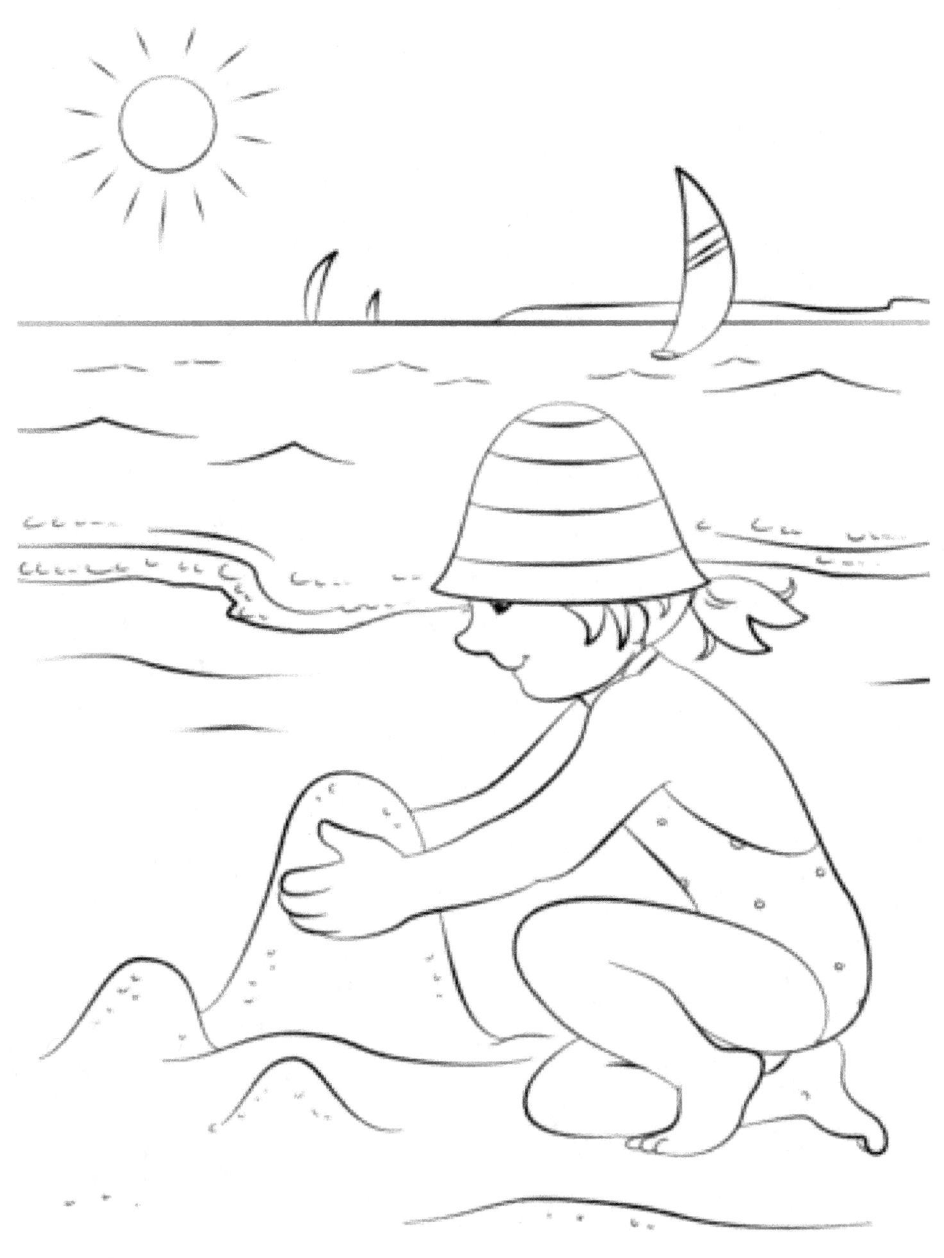

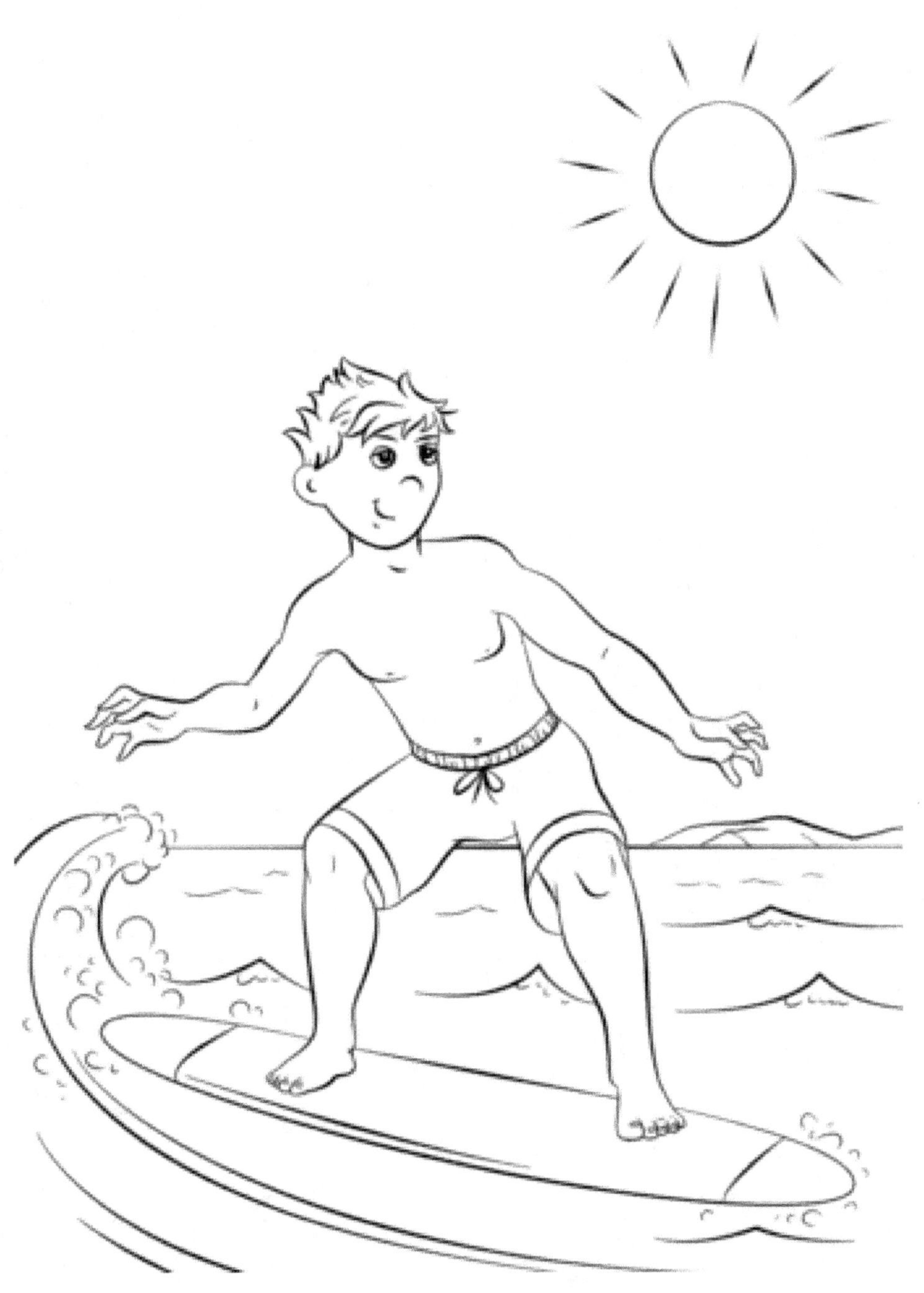

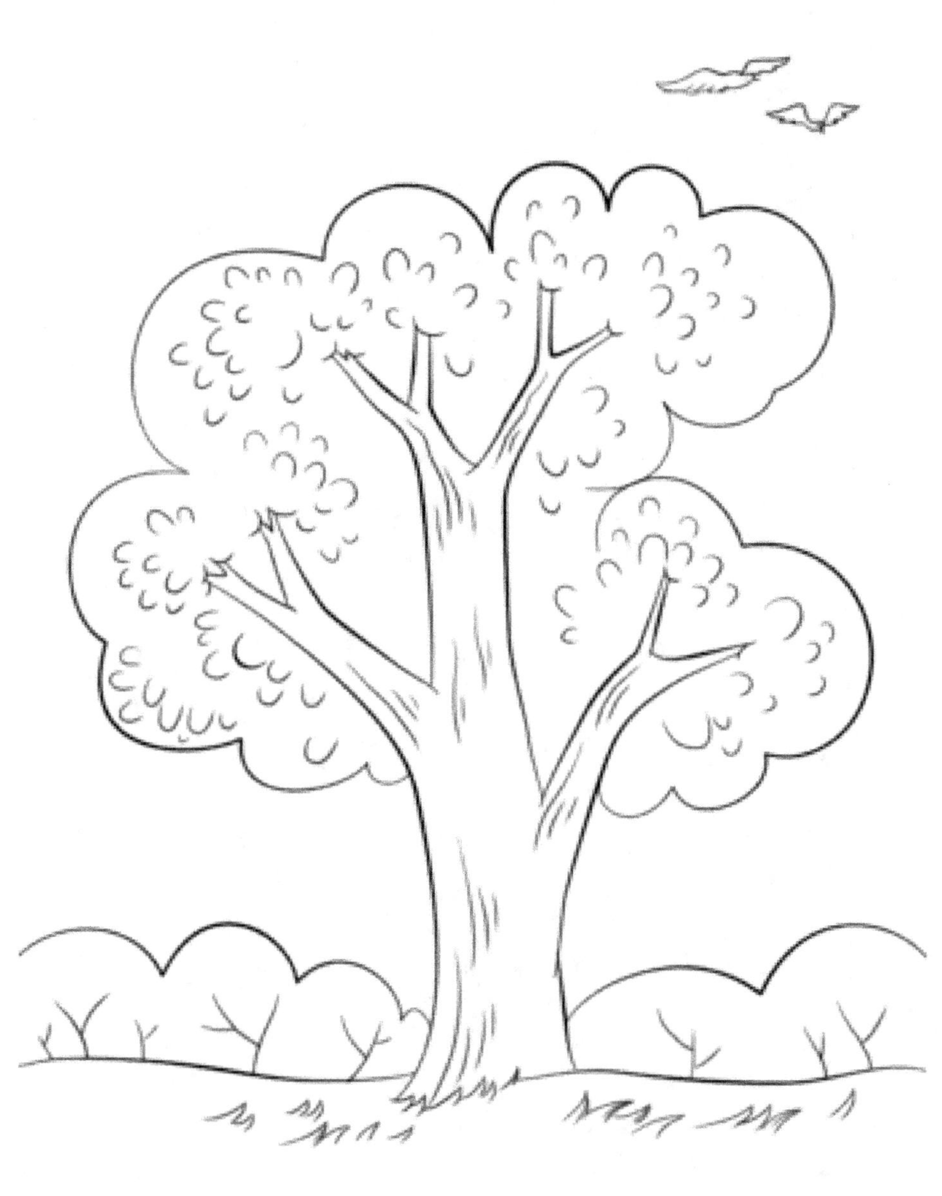

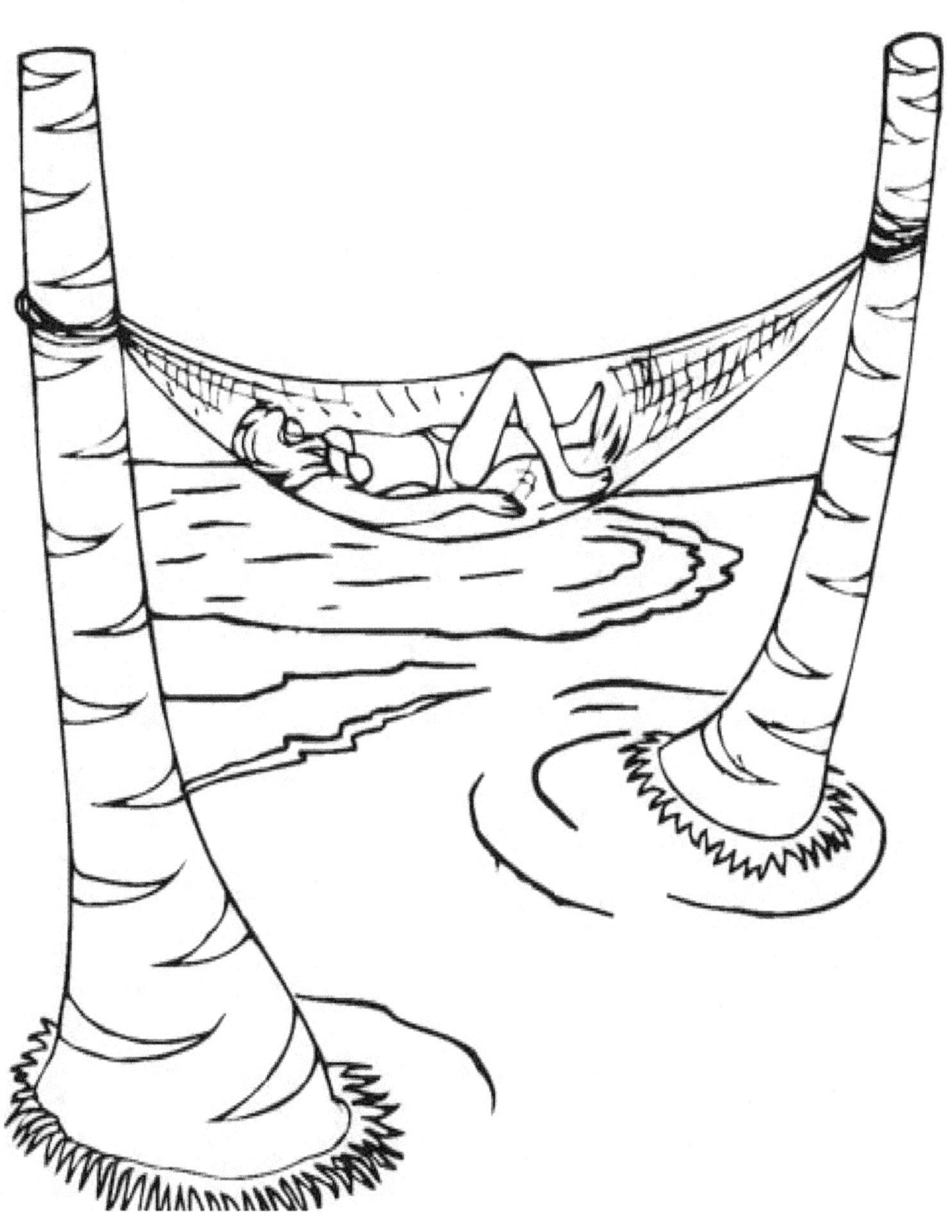

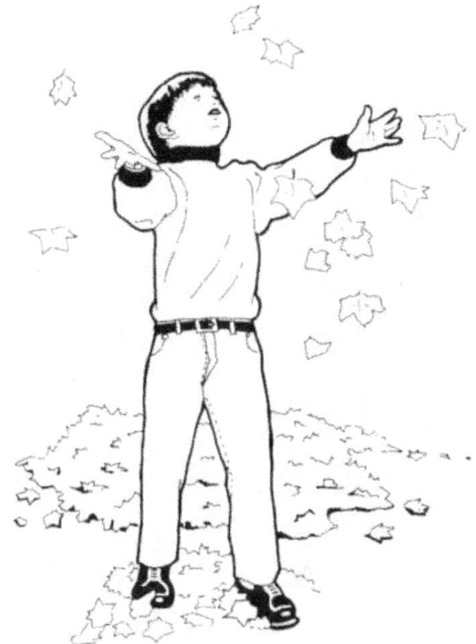

Autumn

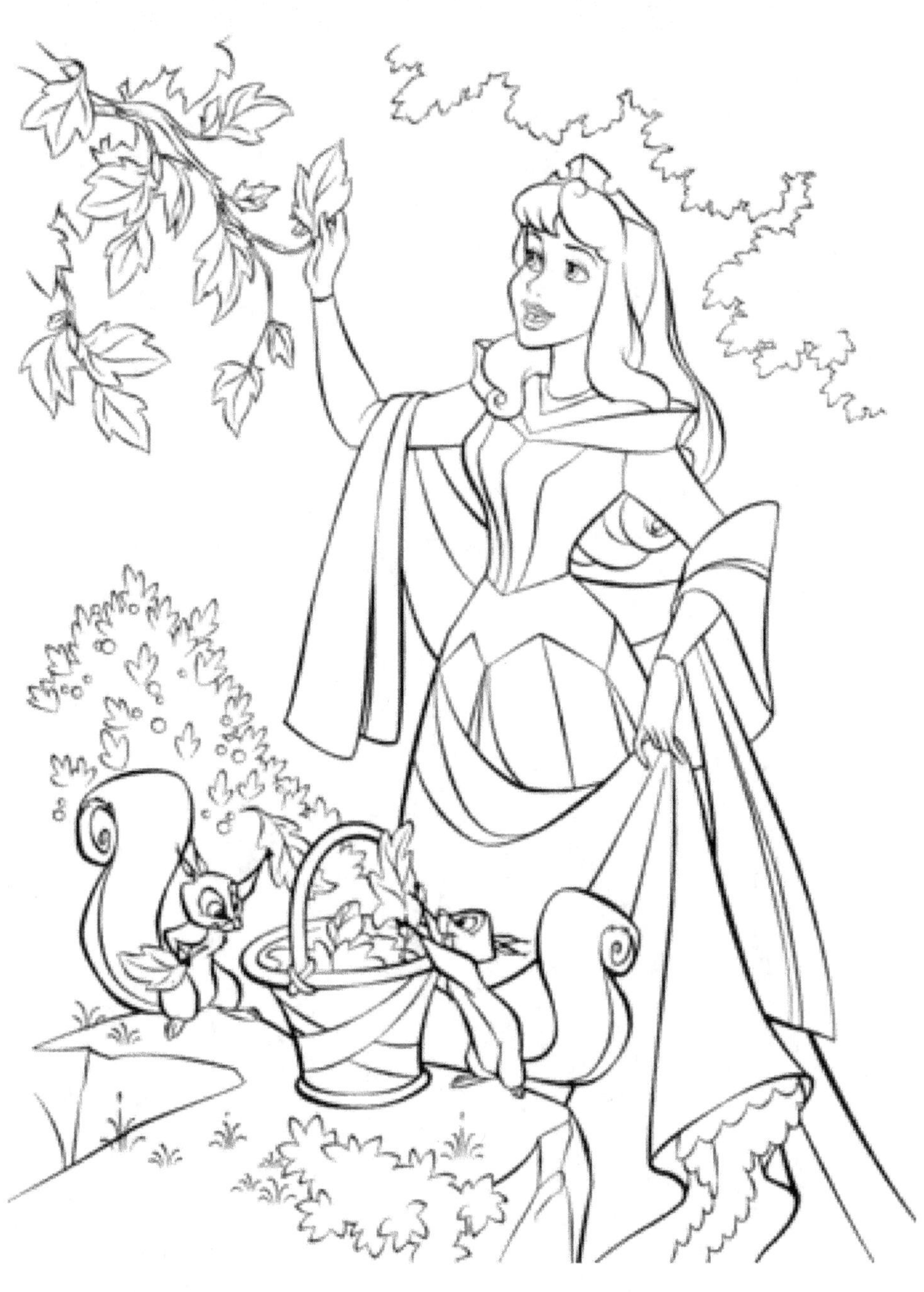

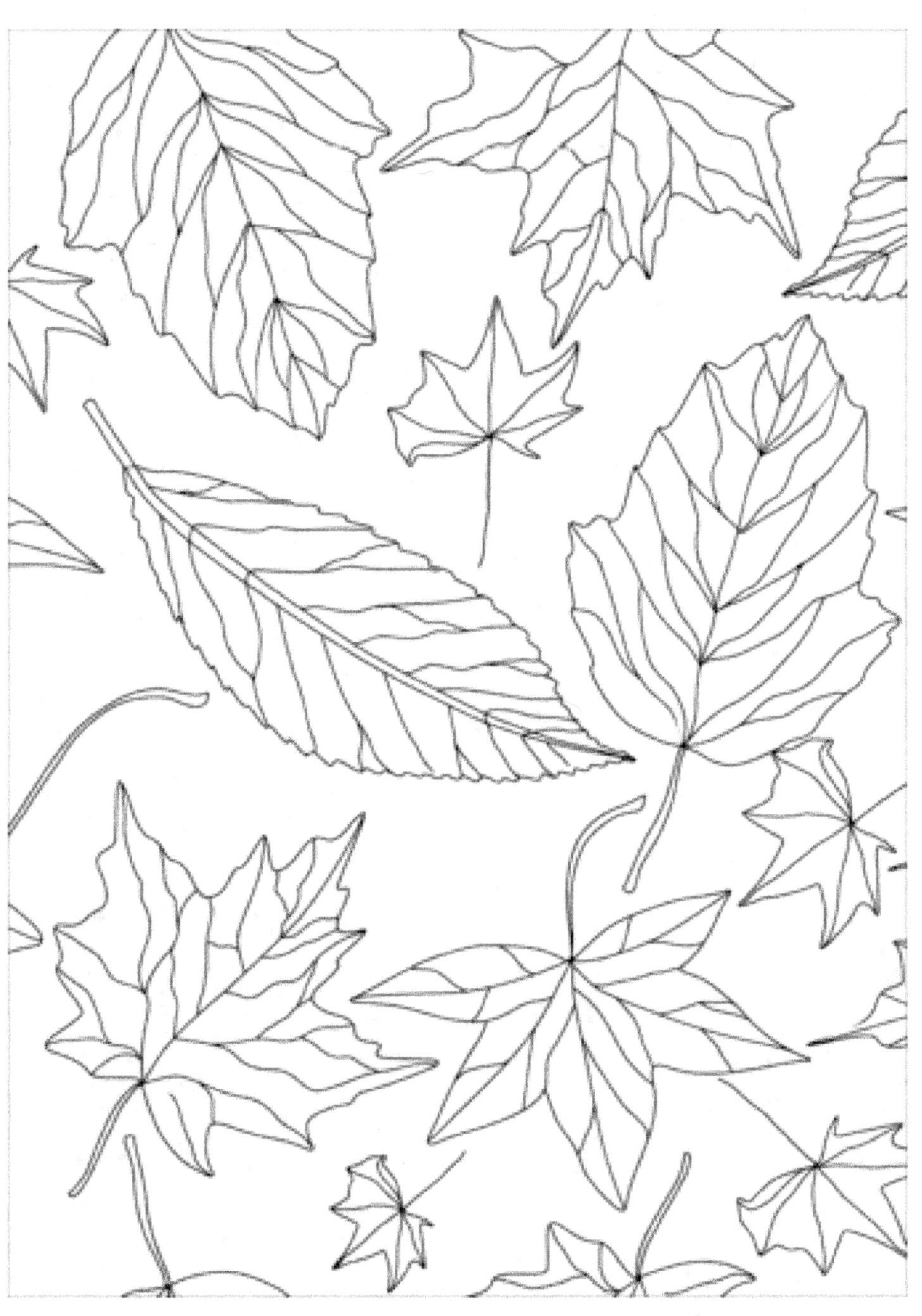

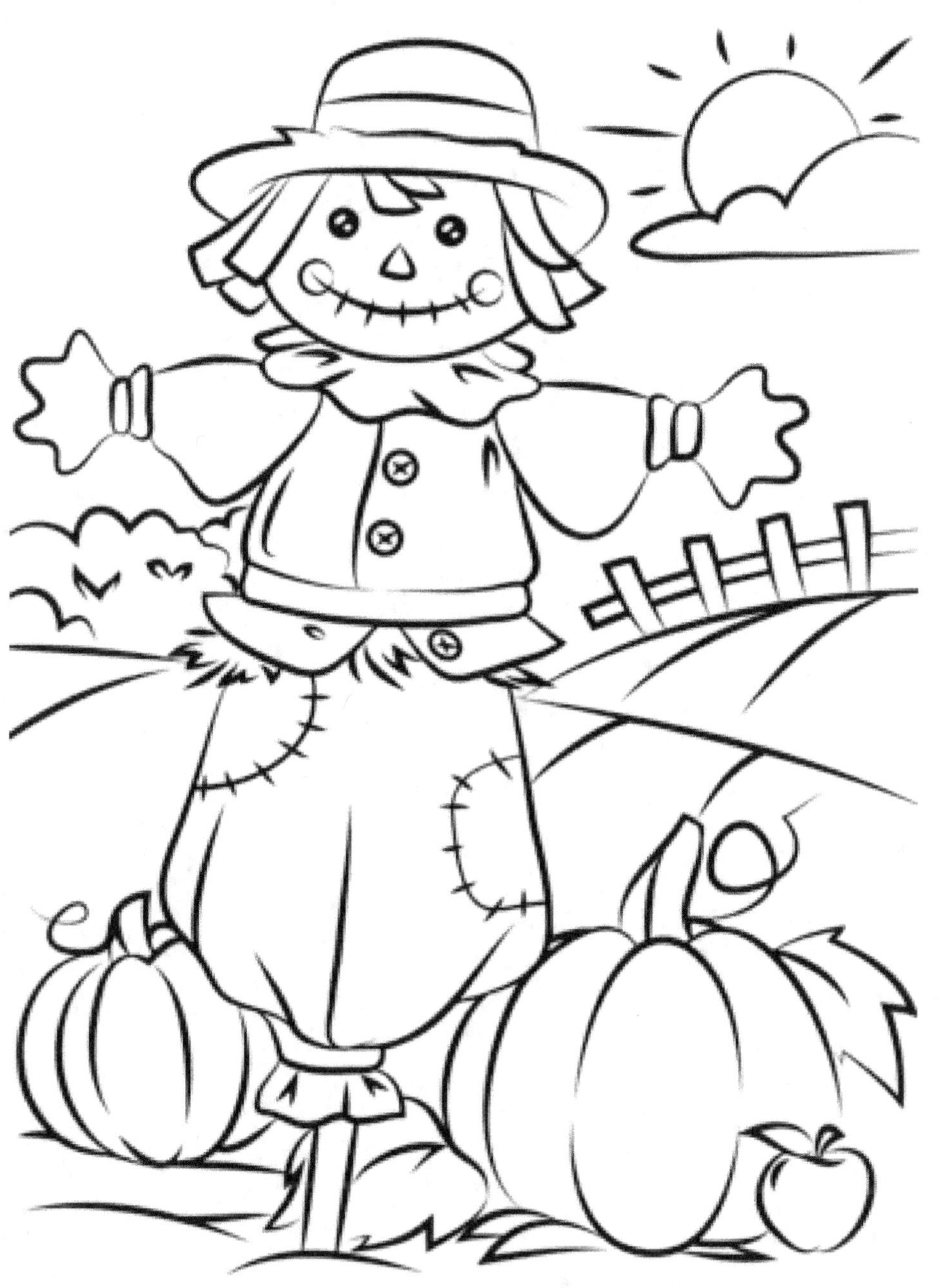

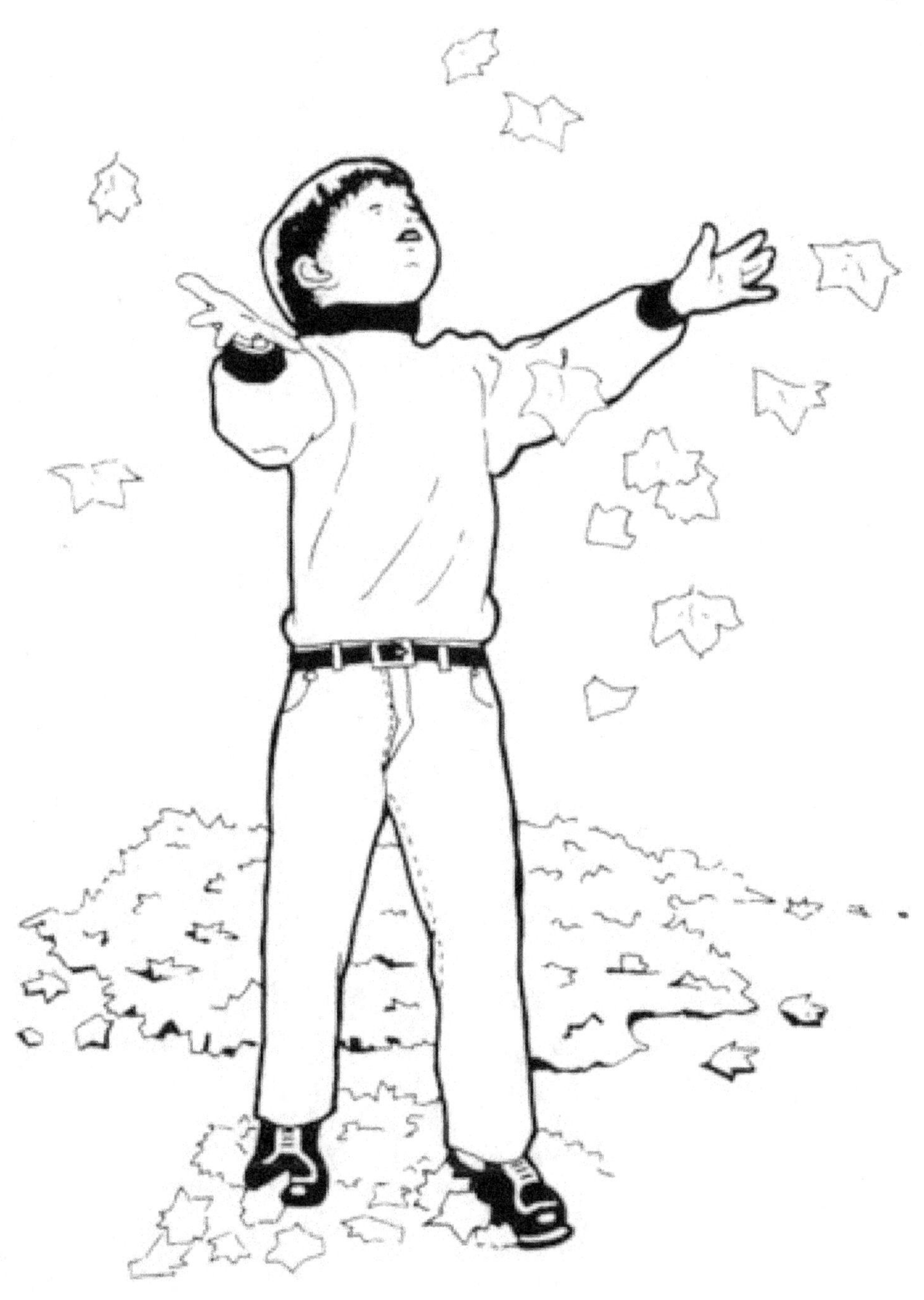

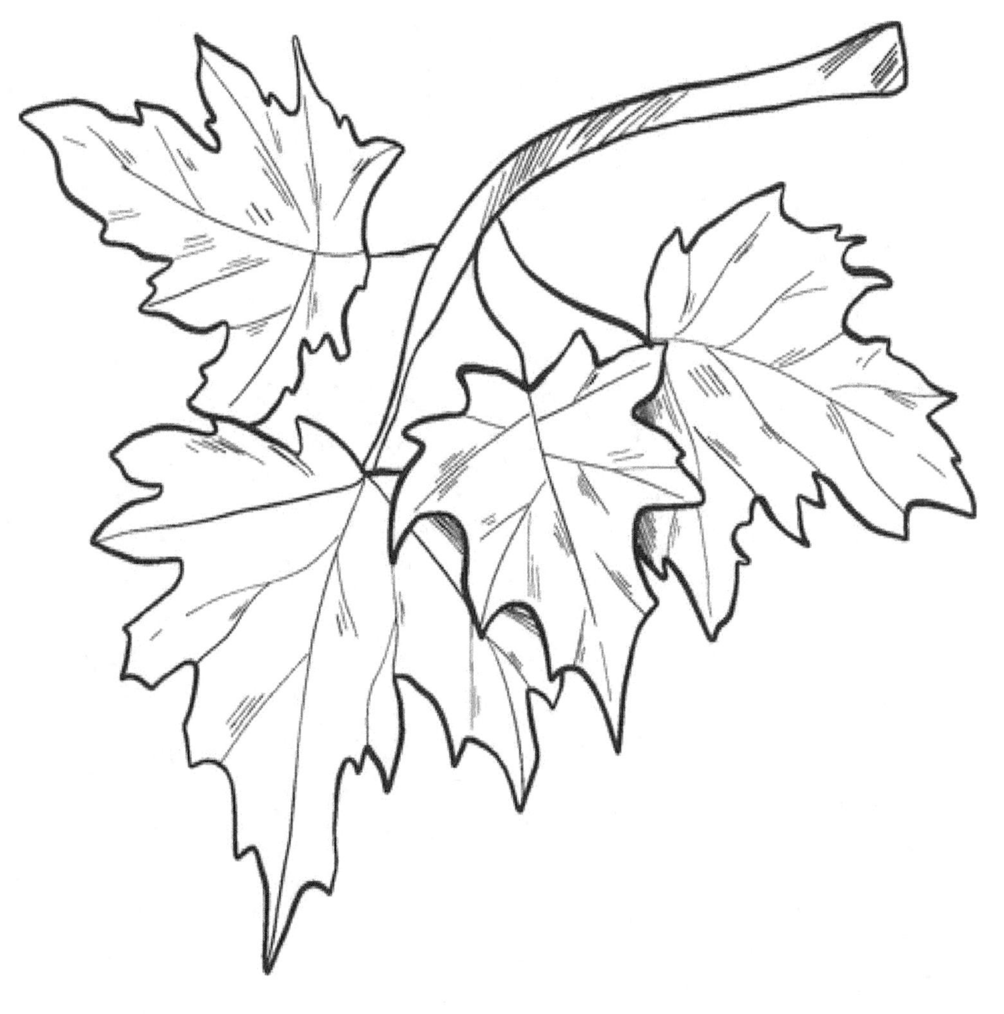

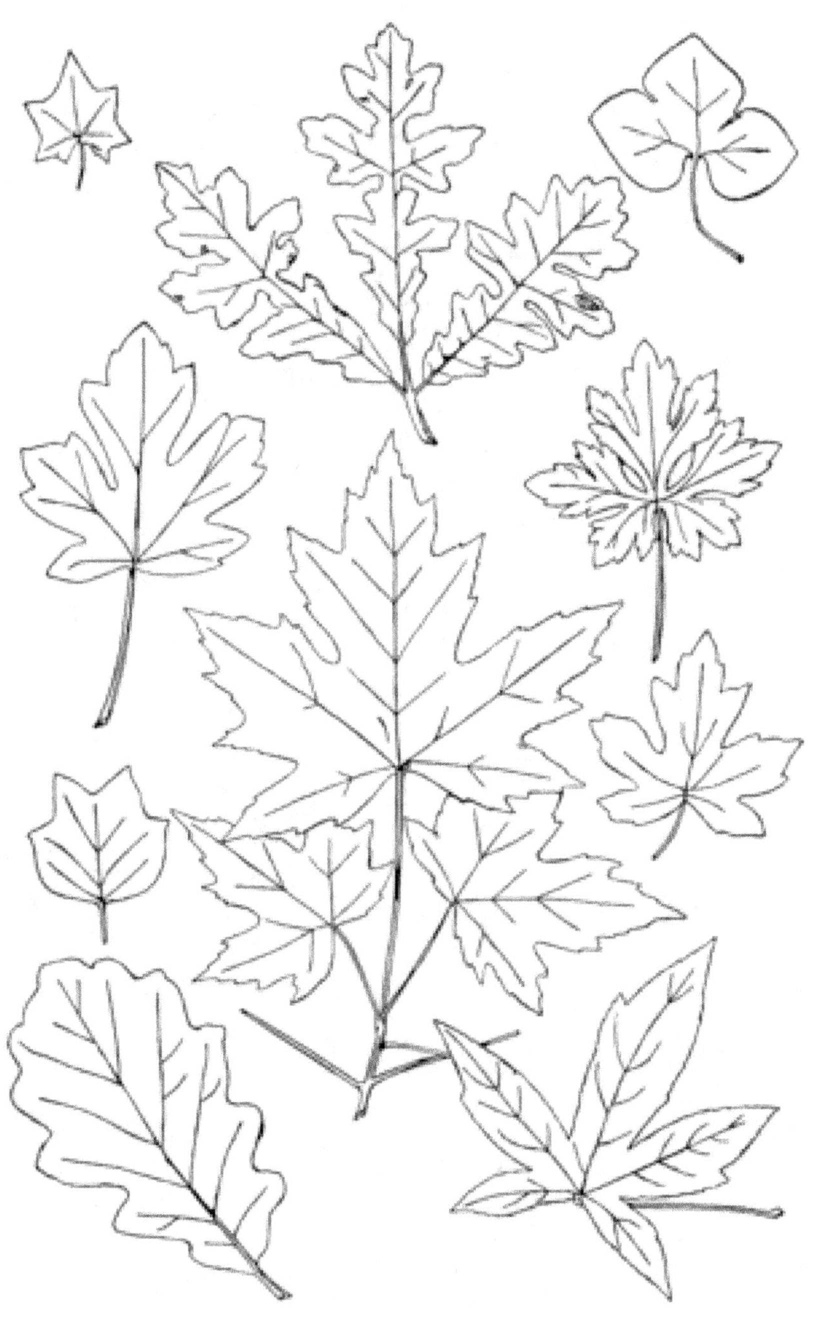

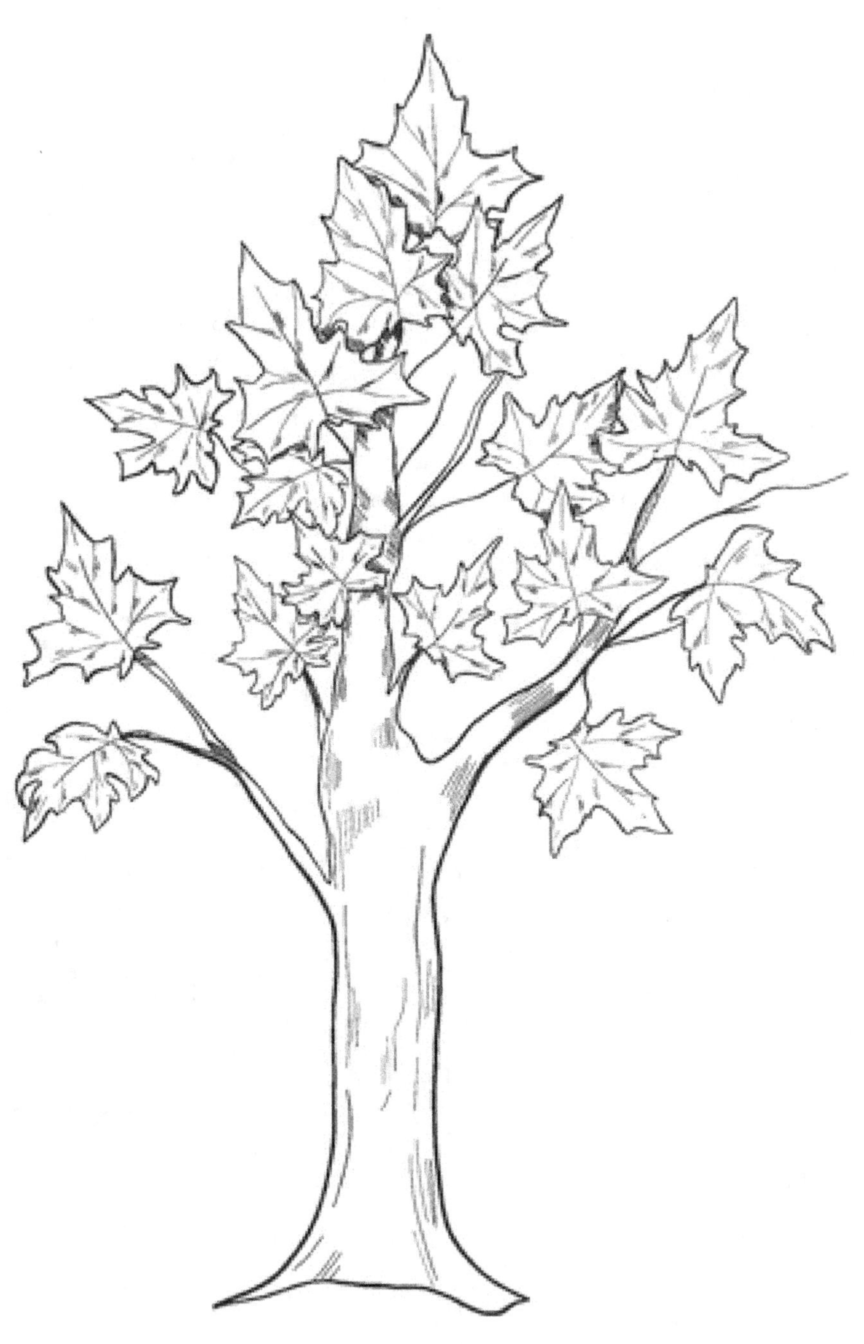

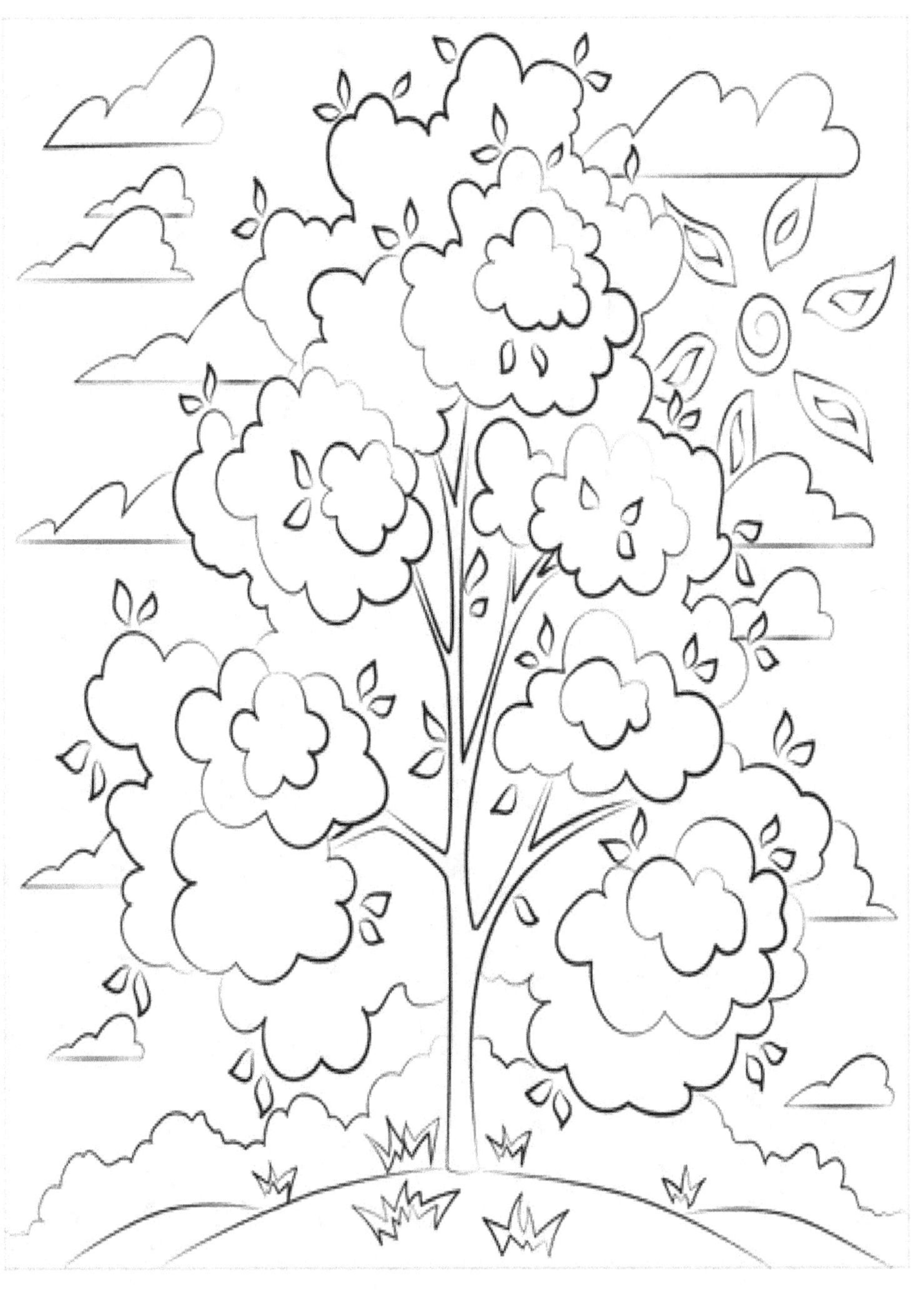

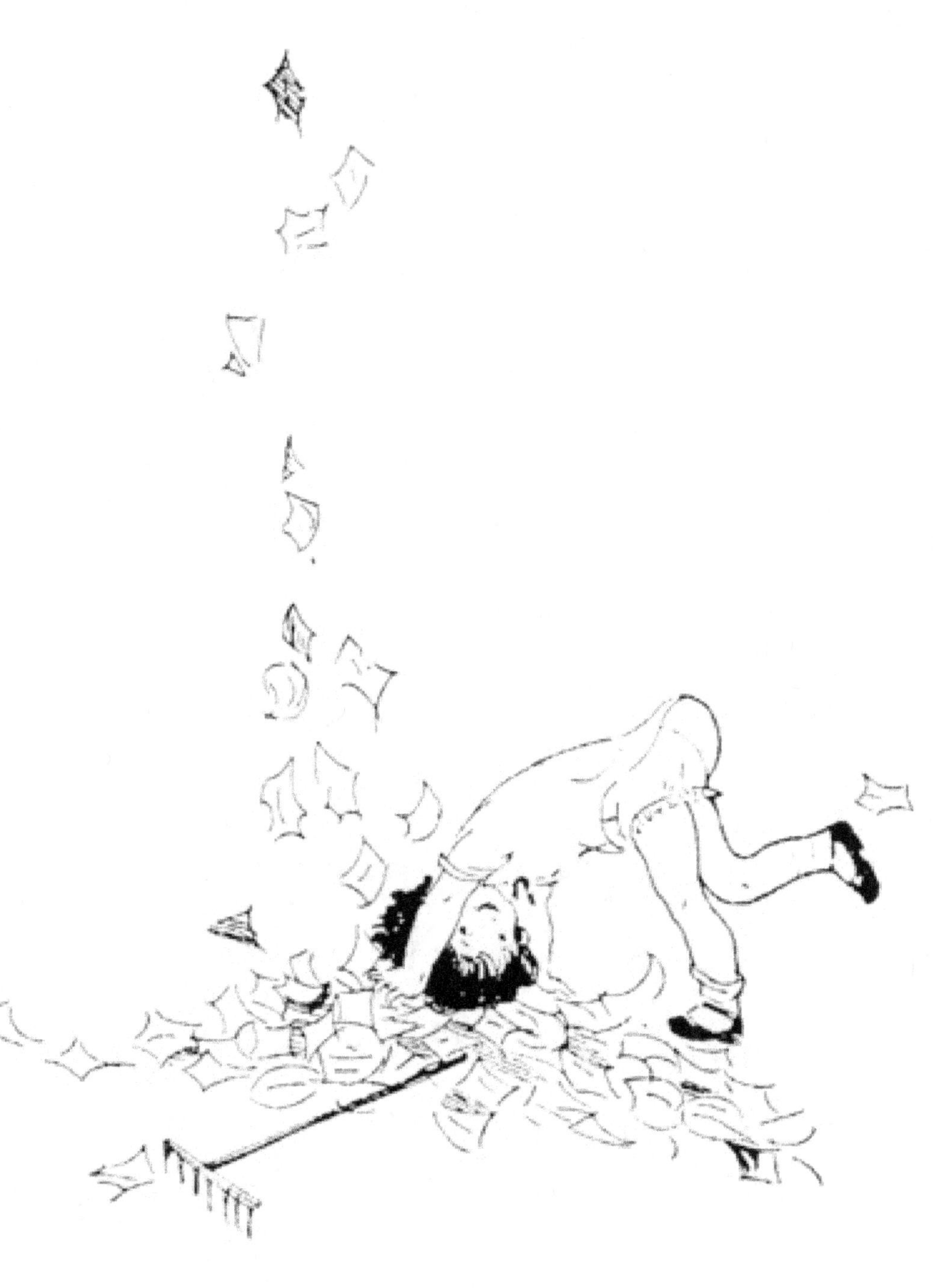

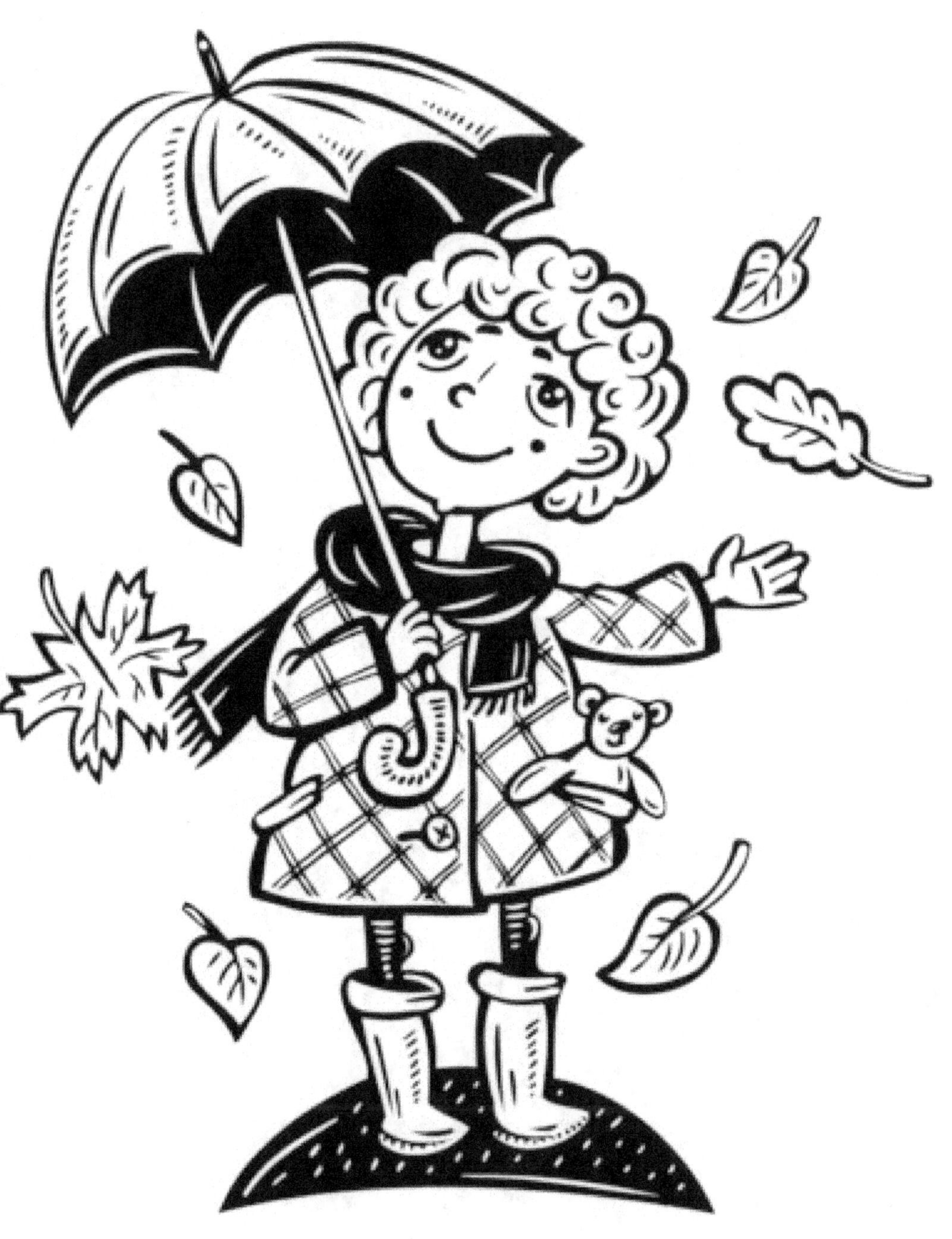

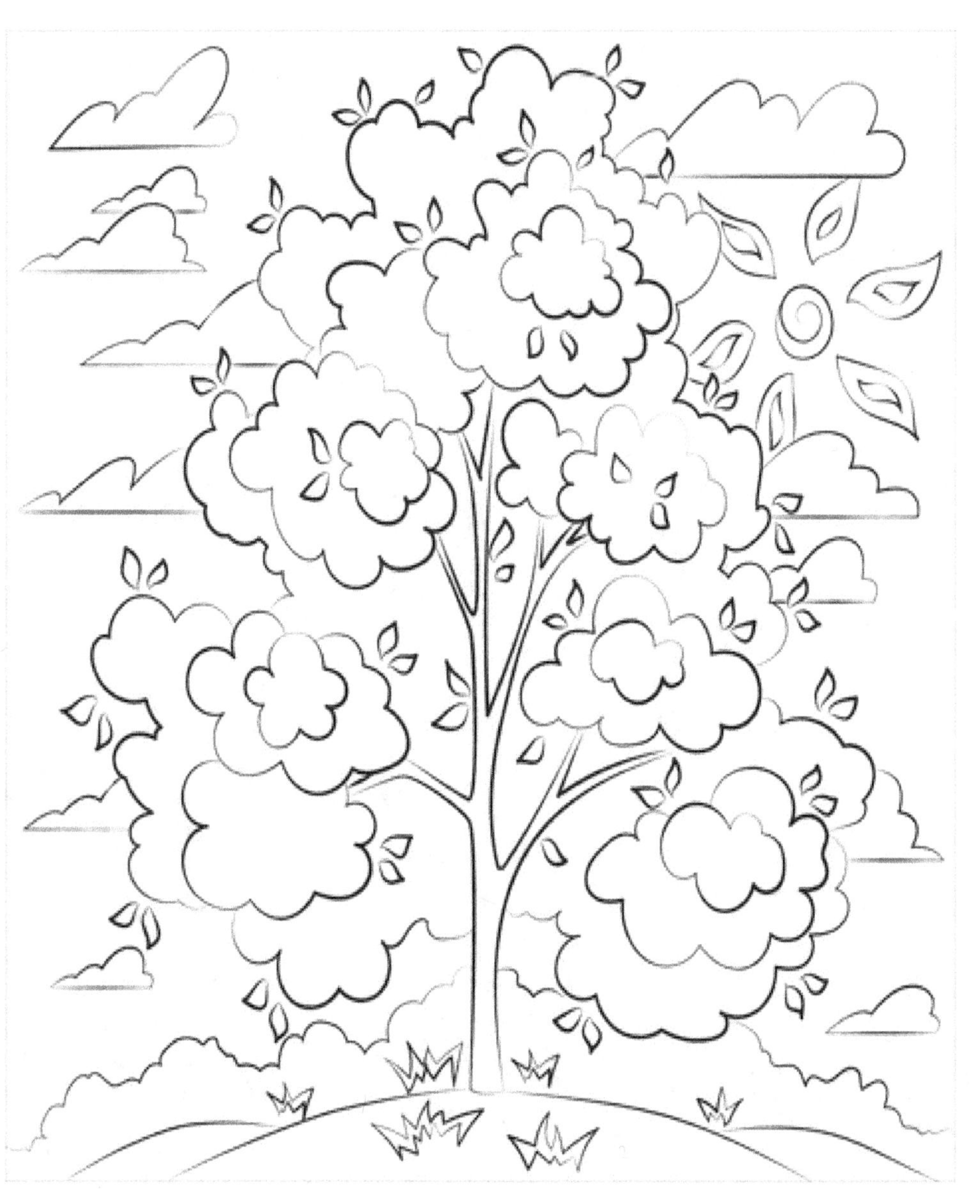

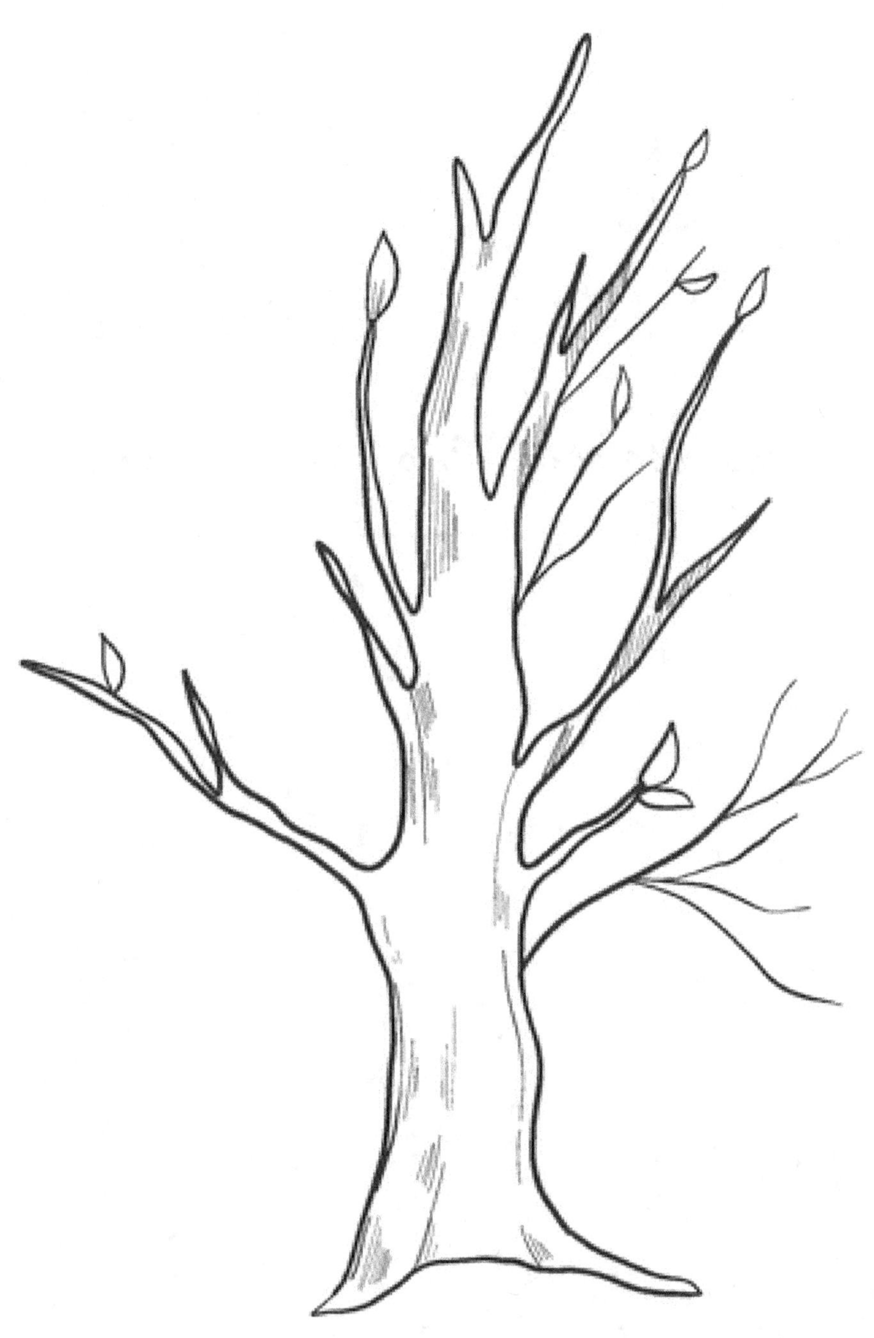

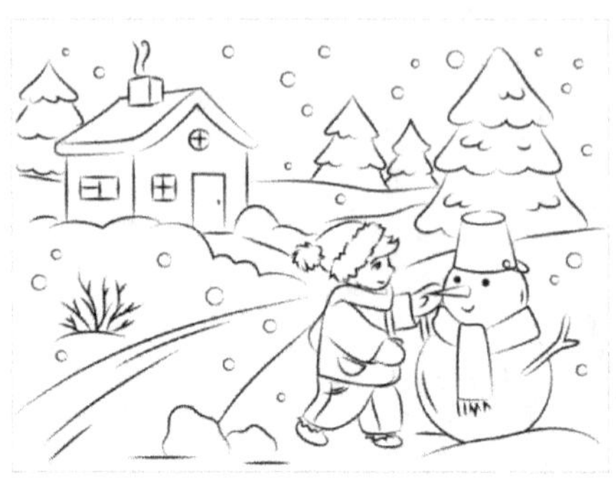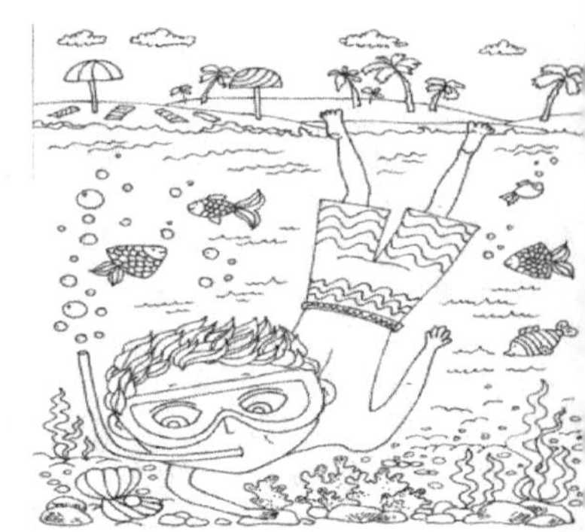

This Coloring Book Belongs to :

____

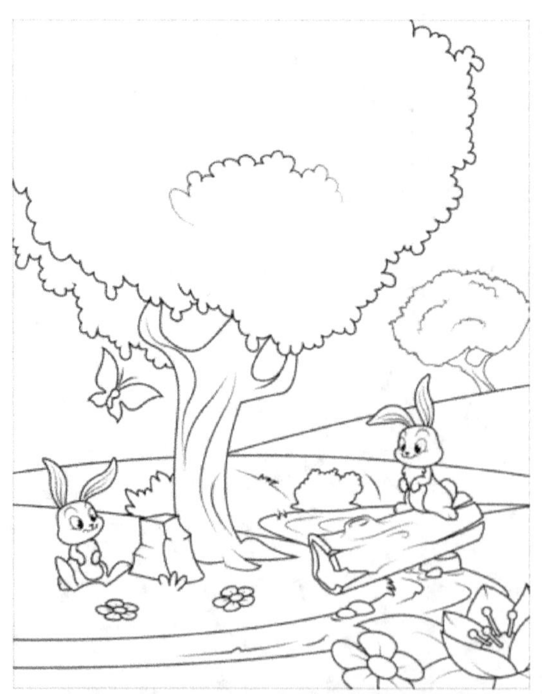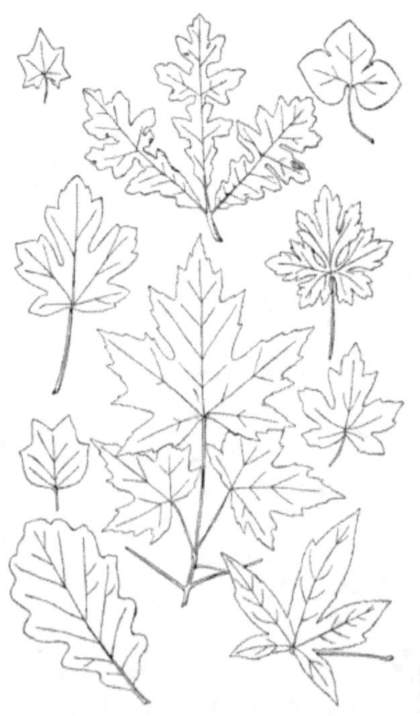

www.ingramcontent.com/pod-product-compliance
Lightning Source LLC
Chambersburg PA
CBHW061459250726
48657CB00005B/1665

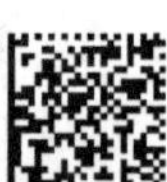

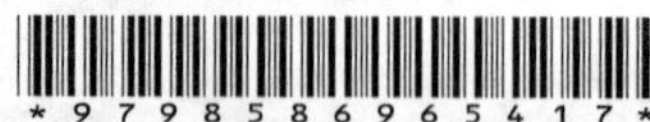